To Don
Best Wishes
Jerome

Also by Jerome Arthur

Antoine Farot and Swede
Down the Foggy Ruins of Time
Life Could be a Dream, Sweetheart
One and Two Halves
The Muttering Retreats
The Death of Soc Smith
The Finale of Seem
Oh, Hard Tuesday
Got no Secrets to Conceal
Brushes with Fame

The Journeyman and the Apprentice

A Novel

Jerome Arthur

To Janet Fardette

The Journeyman and the Apprentice

Published by Jerome Arthur
P.O. Box 818
Santa Cruz, California 95061
831-425-8818
www.JeromeArthurNovelist.com
Jerome@JeromeArthurNovelist.com

Acknowledgments

Thanks to Morton Marcus for editorial assistance. Cover art by Roger DeMoss.

One

Carlos Rángel had been a barber since his late teens, and now twenty-four years later, he was still cutting hair. He had a two-chair set-up that fronted on Cypress Avenue in Cypress Park. The shop was located in what used to be the garage for the house on the hill behind it. He'd bought the house and shop on the G.I. bill when he got out of the Navy at the end of the war nine years ago. The barber he'd bought it from had moved out to Glendale because he wanted to get out of the city. When he left the neighborhood, he also left a clientele that Carlos kept for about five years, but, through attrition and the usual neighborhood turnover, had disappeared for the most part.

When Carlos bought the shop, a barber named Bob Jones worked the second chair. Jonesy, at that point, hadn't yet gone completely to hell from drinking, and he had a pretty good clientele. As the troops came home after the war, the shop got busy and stayed that way for quite a few years. Eventually, the bottle caught up with Jonesy and he started missing work and leaving customers, and Carlos, hanging. Finally, one day he didn't show up at all, but by then business had tapered off for both of them, so it was no problem for Carlos to take Jonesy's customers. Carlos had been working the shop alone ever since.

Now Carlos was spending a lot of his time sitting on a stool at the back of the shop playing his tenor saxophone. About two years ago, when he first realized that business was slowing down, he decided to use his newfound spare time to learn how to play the instrument. It was something he'd always wanted to do, and he was getting good at it. There were contributing factors for the business slowing down. He really needed to get busy remodeling the shop, and he also needed to learn the latest style in men's haircuts, the flat top. He also needed to stop playing his horn when someone walked through the door. That's how lost he got in his music sometimes.

Carlos lived with his wife, Teresa, and nineteen-year-old daughter, Carmela, in the house on the hill above the shop. His widowed mother-in-law, Señora Guevara, who spoke no

The Journeyman and the Apprentice

English, lived in a bungalow a few blocks down the street. He was thirty-five when his own parents died seven years ago. They were both heavy smokers, and they died of smoking related ailments within a year of each other. It was long before that that Carlos himself decided not to smoke. And he never did. From his earliest days he could remember not liking the smell of burned tobacco. The house he grew up in was permeated with it.

Carmela was probably paying the heaviest price for Carlos' slowdown. He barely stayed busy enough to afford a Catholic education for her. The first years after he got home from the war weren't too bad because the shop was busy. It was her high school years, the early 'fifties, that were the roughest. She'd started grammar school at Santa Teresita in the old neighborhood eight months after Carlos joined the Navy and went off to war in the Pacific. She finished grade school at Divine Saviour in Cypress Park and went to high school at Sacred Heart in Lincoln Heights. Business started slowing down for Carlos when Carmela was a sophomore at Sacred Heart, and that was when Teresa got a job as a checker at the Gateway market down on Avenue Twenty-six, one block off Figueroa.

Jerome Arthur

It was really because of Teresa's job that Carmela was able to complete four years at Sacred Heart. Carlos' business was fading rapidly, and Jonesy was spending more and more time in the beer joint down on San Fernando Road, across the street from the train yard. So Teresa worked hard at the market because she wanted Carmela to go to college, but when the time came, there wasn't yet enough money to send her, so Carmela got a job as a typist at Occidental Insurance Company downtown not two months after she graduated from Sacred Heart. Her first semester out of high school, she took evening classes at Los Angeles City College.

On the slow days when he knew it wasn't going to get any better and he needed a break from his sax, Carlos would cross the street to the little corner grocery store and hang out with his friend Enrique Contreras who wasn't very busy, either. Carlos could see his own shop from the grocery store, and he kept an eye on it as he wiled away the midday with his friend. Standing at a certain angle near the front door, he could see John's barber shop two blocks down the street. John had recently put a new sign over his front door. It was a foot high and it stuck out over the sidewalk three feet. It said FLAT TOPS on both sides in bright red letters

The Journeyman and the Apprentice

about eight inches high against a white field.
Just when Carlos got relaxed and started enjoy-
ing his visit, Señora Guevara came into the
store. The minute she laid eyes on him, she said
in her perfect idiomatic Spanish,

"¿Why are you not working, mijito?"

She'd been calling him that since he was
fourteen years old. Señora Guevara had always
treated him with respect and affection and had
loved him as if he were her own son. Plus, she
really didn't mean to imply anything by the
question. Nevertheless, questions like that, especially when they came from her, always made
him feel the pressure.

"'Cause there ain't no negocio right
now, suegra," he replied in his own brand of
Spanish.

She was a slight little woman, but her
size didn't suggest weakness in any way. Carlos
had always been impressed by her strong personality. Her gray hair lent her an air of authority. She wandered off through the narrow aisles
of the tiny grocery store, and Carlos and Enrique picked up their conversation as soon as
she was gone. She bought a pound bag of pinto
beans, a can of Ortega chiles and a half dozen
flour tortillas. Then the two men watched as she
walked off, back toward her house and, after she

11

dropped off her groceries, Divine Saviour. She made an afternoon visit to the church every day to light a votive candle in memory of her late husband.

Carlos looked over at his shop and saw his wife coming down the stairs from the house on her way to work. Like her mother, Teresa was not a big woman. Señora Guevara wasn't overweight, but she was a little heavier than her daughter. Teresa still looked quite young with her long, dark hair and petite figure. Carlos went back across the street. They met in front of his shop. Standing together they were a study in opposites when it came to complexion. Carlos was the lightest, Teresa the darkest. Carmela and her grandmother were somewhere between the two. All three women were beauties.

"See you at dinner, Carlitos," Teresa said.

"Okay, honey."

They kissed and parted. He went up the stairs to the house. From inside he kept an eye on the front door of the shop, although he wasn't sure why he needed to, since nobody went in during the whole time he was up there.

He went to the kitchen and heated some refried beans in a saucepan and made himself a salsa of diced Ortega green chiles, tomatoes and

12

The Journeyman and the Apprentice

onions. Then he heated two flour tortillas over the open flame of the burner on the gas stove. He sat at the dining room table and looked down at the shop while he ate his burritos with whole jalapeño chiles on the side. Two customers had gone into Contreras' place, and they both came out carrying medium size bags of groceries. Carlos was glad to see that at least Contreras was doing some business.

When he stepped back onto the side-walk, Jaime, the old retired hod carrier whose wife had died from cancer just last year, approached. Jaime had lived in the neighborhood for thirty years, up the hill on Isabel Street, and he was one of Señor Guevara's (Carlos' late father-in-law) cronies. As far as Carlos knew, he'd never gone to any other barber shop as long as he'd lived there.

"You got time for a haircut?" he asked as Carlos came face to face with him.

"Sure. Go 'head on in."

He stood aside allowing Jaime to enter ahead of him. Customers like Jaime would always come to Carlos no matter what. His shop, with its worn twenty-year-old barber chairs, waiting chairs with cracked vinyl upholstery taped one time too many, and the water-spotted mirrors, was familiar and comfortable territory for the likes of Jaime, and he would go there even when he didn't need a haircut to hang out in much the same way Carlos had gone across the street before lunch to hang around with Contreras. He'd tell Carlos all about his wife, how wonderful she'd been, how she'd died a slow, painful death. Carlos was getting a little tired of the story, but he listened politely, nevertheless, because he realized that Jaime needed to tell someone. Contreras was a good listener too, and Jaime would sometimes go across the street when he left the barber shop. He'd tell Enrique the same story.

Carlos cut his hair in about twenty minutes and collected a dollar and a quarter for the job. When Jaime left and headed across the street, Carlos swept the floor, picked up a *National Geographic* from the dusty stack on the end table at the rear of the shop, walked back up front, and sat down in his chair in the front window.

At three-thirty after school got out, Rudy, a fifth grader from Divine Saviour sat down in the chair and asked for a butch. Now, that was one Carlos could do. Fifteen minutes later the boy walked out of the shop running his hand over his newly butched head.

The Journeyman and the Apprentice

As Carlos was sweeping the floor, he saw the guy from the *Herald Express* deliver the Eight Star edition to Contreras' store. He put the broom away in the back and crossed the street. He pulled one of the papers out of the metal rack as he entered the store.

Contreras sat like Buddha behind his counter. Carlos grabbed the extra stool and sat down, handing Contreras the front page as he kept the sports section. For the next half hour they read, exchanging sections as they finished reading them. Carlos glanced at his front door from time to time, but no one entered. The OPEN sign in the window glared in the afternoon sun.

"¡Híjola!" Carlos said. "Art Aragón wants to get in the ring with Carmine Basilio."

"Really? Pinchi Metsican's go'n'a get his ass kicked, eh. Ain't no way Golden Boy's go'n'a beat Basilio."

"Es verdad, eh. What the hell, if he thinks he can beat 'im, why not just go 'head on and fight 'im?"

"I guess, but what's in it for Basilio? Ain't no title on the line. How big could the purse be?"

When they finished reading the paper, Contreras put it back together and Carlos walked it outside and put it in the rack. As he re-entered the store, a fifty-three Chevy convertible with four teenagers in it passed by.

"Look at that, eh. Kids, and they got a new car! I ain't got a car. You got a car?" asked the portly grocer, rhetorically.

"Yuh know I ain't got one," Carlos replied. "Can't afford it, eh."

"I can't believe it. Me and you got'a take the streetcar, and they got their own car. Ain't no justice."

"Rich gavachos from Eagle Rock. Prob'ly their father's car."

Carlos stayed and talked with Enrique until almost five o'clock when a young man he'd never seen around the neighborhood before approached his front door. He said so long to the grocer and crossed the street. The stranger had entered on his own, and Carlos arrived at the door right after it closed. He opened it and went in to find the stranger standing in the middle of the shop looking around.

"Hi, need a haircut?"

"Yeah."

"Have a seat right here."

Carlos picked up the haircloth and indicated with his open right hand for the young man to sit.

16

The Journeyman and the Apprentice

"How yuh want it?" he asked.

"Longer in back so I can have a duck tail. Square it on the neck?"

"How yuh want the sideburns?"

"Leave 'em long. And just trim the top."

"You live around here?" Carlos asked as he began cutting the hair. "Ain't never seen yuh before."

"I live up in Glassell Park near Saint Bernard's. I go by here every day on the street-car on my way to work and back home."

"Really? Where yuh work?"

"Clifton's Cafeteria on Broadway. I see your shop all the time from the streetcar. Wanted to stop for a haircut, but never had time."

"What's your name?"

"Peter. You Carlos?"

"That's right. How long yuh been working at Clifton's?"

"Couple years but it's only temporary. I'm lookin' for somethin' better."

"Pay pretty good?"

"Nah. Best parta' the job, y'r meals'er included, and the food's good."

And so the conversation went for twenty minutes. Barber shop small talk, Carlos called it. When he finished the haircut and got his dollar and a quarter, he did his last clean-up for the day, and got ready to close up.

He fooled around with his horn till a quarter to six. That was when Carmela got off the streetcar and poked her head in the front door. She was a younger version of her mother and grandmother small, dark (but not quite as dark as Teresa), and beautiful. Carlos thought his daughter looked a little like Rita Moreno. On those nights when she didn't have a class at City, her arrival home was Carlos' signal to turn the sign around, lock the front door and count the money in the till. He only made seven dollars and twenty-five cents that day. Five haircuts for a dollar and a quarter, and one, the boy because he was under twelve, for a dollar. No tips.

He stood over the sink and splashed warm water on his face. As he blotted himself dry with the hand towel, he looked in the mirror. His dark brown eyes looked weary, incipient crow's feet at the corners. He'd always thought the slow days made him more tired than the busy ones. His black hair was still thick and full on top, but it was getting gray at the temples. His mustache was getting gray, too.

He took his saxophone upstairs. As he entered the living room, he could see Carmela through the kitchen door starting dinner. After

18

The Journeyman and the Apprentice

he got his slippers on, he sat at the dining room table, and talked to his daughter.

"How was your day?" he asked.

"Pretty hectic, but not boring for that reason. I typed correspondence all day. I bet I'm typing sixty to eighty words a minute."

"'Sounds like you're gettin' good."

He felt guilty when he heard how hard she worked. It made him feel like he wasn't holding up his end. But it also motivated him temporarily. Once again, he thought briefly about remodeling the shop.

Teresa arrived at six-fifteen. She went to the bathroom and cleaned up for dinner. When she came out, the shrimp salad Carmela had been fixing was ready.

As they ate dinner, Carlos said to Teresa, "Store busy?"

"Real busy. How 'bout your shop?"

"Just the opposite. Real slow."

"Too badt."

"I *did* pick up a new customer at the end of the day. A young kid from over in Glassell Park. Says he's go'n'a come back next time. Who knows? Maybe my luck's changing, and I'm go'n'a start getting busy again. Oh, by the way, I saw your mother over Enrique's store earlier, just before you left for work."

"Oh, how is Grandma?" Carmela asked. "I haven't seen her since Sunday Mass."

"She's doing good."

"She came by the Gateway after her church visit," Teresa said. "I was too busy to talk to her. She left when she saw I couldn't talk. You comeen to walk home with me tonight?"

It was October, and the days were getting shorter, the time of year when Carlos began taking his late-night walks to the Gateway to meet Teresa and walk her home.

"I'll be there. Wan'a go, Carmela?"

"Sí, Papá."

They finished eating in silence, and then Teresa headed back to work. As Carmela studied in her room, Carlos sat next to his radio in the living room and tuned in to his favorite jazz station out of South-Central Los Angeles. After a while he turned the radio off and practiced on his horn. At nine-thirty he and Carmela were out the door.

Teresa's night had been just as busy as her afternoon, and she was talking a mile a minute, telling them about it on the walk home.

"I'm so tiredt," she said. "Better to be busy 'cause it goes by quick."

"Always said that about my job."

20

The Journeyman and the Apprentice

"The big news today was we're getteen a new manager. They're transferreen Mister Delbert to another store. It's been a rumor for a while, but they madte it official today. I hope the new manager is as goodt as Mister Delbert."

They got back home at ten-fifteen. They listened to the last few minutes (mostly sports and weather) of the late news on the radio. Teresa and Carmela turned in at ten-thirty. Carlos wasn't sleepy, so he decided to go out for a walk before going to bed.

He headed down Cypress, and when he got to John's shop, he stopped and looked in. It was clean as a pin. John had recently painted and put down a new floor. His sinks and chairs were old, but cleaned-up and in good shape, and they looked good in the re-decorated setting. His and Bob's licenses hung above their backbars in glass frames with their names engraved on them in old English lettering. His magazines were stacked neatly on the table next to his waiting chairs. Carlos stepped back and looked at the new sign hanging over John's door.

"Got'a learn how to do flat tops," he mumbled to himself.

He turned and headed back home. It was eleven-thirty when he re-entered the quiet house. He went into the bathroom, washed his face and brushed his teeth. Then he went into the bedroom and stood in the darkness, listening to Teresa's even sleep-breathing for a couple of minutes before climbing into the bed next to her. As he did so, he disturbed her into consciousness, and she said,

"Where didt you go?"

"Took a walk. Went down and looked at John's shop. He's fixed it up. Looks real nice. Got'a start thinking about redecorating."

"Yes, you shouldt, and I couldt halp."

"Only problem is where'm I go'n'a get the cash? Ain't got it. Damn sure ain't making it."

"I can halp," Teresa said.

"Don't wan'a spend your money. You're a real sweetheart for offering, but you should use your money for yourself and for Carmela."

"Listen, we been together too long to start divideen our money up now. It's not my money; it's our money."

"But it would make me too dependent on you."

"We're dependent on each other. We're in this together, and right now I think we got'a get your barber shop goeen again. Only way to do it is together. After we fix it up, you'll be busy again."

The Journeyman and the Apprentice

"Makes sense. I still don't like the idea of not doin' it all myself. Guess I ain't got a choice. Right?"

"Carlitos, mi querido, we got'a get you busy again, and this is the only way."

He knew she was right, but he still resisted in his heart. He couldn't resist out loud anymore, so he was silent, and after a little while they both drifted off to sleep.

Two

The next morning when Carlos awoke, he still had good intentions, but by the time he opened up, he'd all but forgotten his late-night conversation with Teresa. It was Friday and the shop got busy, so he couldn't really think about anything other than the task at hand. The last customer of the morning left at half past eleven. He took a tally of his morning's work and discovered that he'd already done more than he'd done all day Thursday. He did the same in the afternoon, which made that the busiest day he'd had in a long time. And to his further surprise, he was just that busy again on Saturday. Suddenly, he was flush, and he forgot all about remodeling.

On Sunday morning the Rángel family walked down to Señora Guevara's house, and the four of them went to nine o'clock Mass. Señora Guevara and Carmela walked together and talked the whole time in Spanish. Teresa was

The Journeyman and the Apprentice

pleased to see her mother and her daughter getting on so well. They seemed to do so much better together than she did with either one of them. Her mother wanted to tell her what to do and how to run her life, and her daughter wasn't too far removed from the adolescent desire to symbolically kill her the way psychologists say all offspring have a subconscious desire to do.

They got to the church five minutes before Mass started. When the ushers passed the collection basket, Carlos put in a dollar, the first time he'd contributed in over a month. He was feeling generous after the two good days he'd had. The whole family received Holy Communion. After the priest blessed the congregation, "Pax Dominus vobiscum," and the altar boy responded, "Et cum spiritu tuo," the Rángels made their way up the aisle to the vestibule and out the door to the sidewalk in front. They lingered for a few minutes and chatted with other parishioners. Spanish and English wafted on the Sunday morning breeze as though it were all one language.

They walked back home, and Teresa and her mother made a breakfast of huevos rancheros. As they worked in the kitchen, Carmela sat down at the piano, Carlos picked up his horn, and they played some Dave Brubeck and Paul

Desmond. Carlos couldn't quite get his tenor high enough to sound like Paul Desmond's alto, but it didn't matter; he was having a good time. After breakfast they relaxed in the front room and chatted for a while as Carmela played softly in the background. When Señora Guevara left at eleven-thirty, Carmela walked her home. Then she went to her best friend Gloria's house.

Carmela and Gloria had been friends since grammar school. They'd stayed close all the way through Sacred Heart High. Gloria's father was a concrete finisher with steady work, so that made her parents a little better off than Carlos and Teresa. She didn't have to get a job and was able to go to City College full-time. She *did* have a job on the line at a plastics factory in East Los Angeles the last two summers since she graduated from high school.

"I didn't see you at Mass," Carmela said to Gloria after she greeted Señor and Señora Roybal. The two young women went into Gloria's room.

"I went to early Mass because my father doesn't like sitteen through the sermon. I think I wouldt rather put up with the sermon and not have to wake up so early on Sunday."

"You should've come with us."

26

The Journeyman and the Apprentice

"Maybe next Sunday, if Papá insists on getteen up so early. But I really shouldt go with him and Mamá at whatever time they want. They're doeen so much for me. I owe it to them. Papá says I don't have to work next summer. I'm starteen at State in the fall."

"That's great. I wish I could go with you. I'll be twice as long as you at City. I wish I could go full-time. Night school's no fun."

"Lota' cute guys in the daytime."

For such a pretty young woman, Carmela hadn't had much experience going out with boys. She'd only gone to a few dances when she was in high school, but never with a boy, always with Gloria. She'd dance if asked, but she was really quite introverted when it came down to it. Gloria was the extrovert of the two, but neither of them had ever had a boyfriend.

"You met some nice boys?" Carmela asked.

"There's a really cute one in my English class. Bill Rojas. We sit next to each other. He's twenty-two. Got a part-time job in the stock room at the Sears store over near my summer job. Used to be full-time, but he switched to part-time just this semester so he couldt go to school full-time."

"I should talk to him. Maybe he could give me some ideas on how to do it."

"Hey," Gloria said suddenly. "You want to go to Van de Kamp's for Cokes?"

"Sure."

They left Gloria's house, walked to the streetcar line on Cypress Avenue and caught the Five Eagle Rock. The front door of the barber shop was open when they passed Carmela's house, and she saw her father inside mopping the floor. When she looked above at the house, she saw her mother sitting on the couch by the living room window working her knitting needles. They coasted along past the Ralston Purina factory on the left and through the section where the street narrows, crowded on the right by the hill. They got off at Division Street and walked the last mile to the drive-in.

All the drive-up spaces on two sides of the restaurant were packed with cars filled with teenagers and being tended by carhops. All the booths on the inside were filled, too. There were two unoccupied stools at the end of the counter. Carmela and Gloria sat there, looking down the long counter and at the row of booths along the windows that looked out at the cars in the drive-up spots.

The Journeyman and the Apprentice

Carmela ordered a chocolate root beer, Gloria a cherry Coke. They were sitting opposite a booth that was occupied by two young men. As she took her seat, Carmela could see that one of the boys had been following her with his eyes from the moment she'd walked through the door. Their eyes met only briefly, and Carmela looked away quickly, but he kept watching.

"That young man is staring at us," she told Gloria.

"Not us, you. I think he likes you."

When she looked at him again, he was smiling broadly. Then he was sliding out of his seat in the booth and moving toward them. He had dark hair, blue eyes and a light complexion. Before Carmela could even think of a response to Gloria's statement, the young man was sitting on the stool next to her. A very fat man who'd finished eating a double cheeseburger and a dinner-plate-size stack of onion rings had just given it up. The young man pushed the dishes aside, and, using the discarded paper napkin that was crumpled up next to the plate, he wiped dry a puddle left by a sweating glass of ice water.

"Hi, my name's Jack Niel. What's yours?" he asked with a broad smile still on his face.

Jerome Arthur

Carmela was so taken aback that she was momentarily speechless. Her dark eyes gazed into his baby blues. She'd never been approached like this before, and she honestly didn't know what to do. Gloria was a little more daring than Carmela, and she spoke right up.

"Her name's Carmela and mine's Gloria. It's nice to meet you, Jack."

His smile got broader, and he nodded at the two ladies. His friend was watching from the booth.

"Would you girls like to join us in our booth? We got room."

"We'd be delightedt," Gloria said.

Carmela just went along, but not before giving Gloria a puzzled look.

Jack stood up and turned to the booth. He held his right arm out the way an usher would at a wedding. As the women approached the table, Jack said,

"Carmela, Gloria, this is Raúl Medina."

Carmela was struck by how excellent Jack's Spanish pronunciation was.

Raúl said, "It's just Raul. Jack here's just showing off."

They all exchanged hellos and began to get acquainted.

30

The Journeyman and the Apprentice

"So, you girls live around here?" Jack asked.

"Cypress Park," Gloria replied. "You?"

"Glassell Park," Raul said. "Still liveen at home. Jack's got himself a pad over off Fig by Mount Washington."

"Both of us still live at home," Gloria said. "We're students at L.A.C.C."

Since Carmela was only a part-time student, she didn't think Gloria was being completely truthful, so she gave her the same look she gave her when she accepted the invitation to the booth, but she didn't say anything. She let her go on. When they finished their sodas, Jack suggested that they all go for a ride in his car. Carmela was hesitant, but Gloria was eager, and she talked Carmela into it.

The two young men stood next to the booth as the women slid out. When they were all standing, Jack reached over to the hat rack and grabbed by the brim a white Panama fedora with a black ribbon. Outside the restaurant, they crossed the parking lot to a 'thirty-nine Chevy. The car was so old and beat-up that Carmela doubted it would take them anywhere, much less bring them back.

"Don't look like much," Jack said when he saw her apprehension, "but it runs real good."

The two guys were complete gentlemen. Jack unlocked the passenger doors and held the front one for Carmela as Raul held the back for Gloria. Then he drove down San Fernando Road heading toward downtown.

"How about we go down the Placita and check out the mariachis? We could go over Olvera Street for taquitos later."

Jack's pronunciation of the Spanish words continued to be near perfect in the Mexican dialect, prompting Gloria to say,

"You speak Spanish very well. Where didt you learn it?"

"Hangin' around with vatos like Raul here, and some a' my Navy camaradas. Mi carnal in the Navy was a chicano. Lot I picked up from him. Used to go on leave together. Didn't have no home of my own to go to, so I'd stay with him and his family. His mom and dad don't speak no English. I was forced to learn it if I wanted to talk to them."

"Your Spanish is better than your English," Carmela said. "What did you say your last name was?"

32

The Journeyman and the Apprentice

"Niel. It's French. Spelled N-I-E-L. No-tice how I pronounce it Nee él? That's the French pronunciation. When I started school, teachers were always wantin' to pronounce it Neel, and I was always correcting 'em. This way it sounds more like a Mexicano name."

They drove down North Broadway through Chinatown, turned left on Sunset, went down to Alameda, and parked across the street from Union Station. They walked through Olvera Street to get to the Placita where mari-achis played. The atmosphere was festive, the women dressed in bright reds and contrasting blacks, the men in western-cut gabardine trou-sers, long-sleeve white shirts, well-polished cowboy boots, fancy white straw hats with the brims curled up on the sides and a thin leather lariat hanging from the brim to below the nape. Little children cavorted in their Sunday best, speaking Spanish. The two couples sat down on a bench and watched the festivities.

After a while they went back to Olvera Street where they mingled with the tourists and stood in line at one of the many stands that sold taquitos. When they finished eating, they went back to the car and cruised down Broadway to Eighth Street and doubled back up Hill Street,

North Broadway and Figueroa to Cypress Avenue.

Even though she was reticent to go with these boys at first, Carmela had to admit that she'd had a good time with them. She didn't have to ask Gloria if she'd enjoyed herself. She could see from her constant banter that she, too, was delighted to have spent the afternoon with these young men. When they pulled up in front of Carmela's house, Jack asked,

"Whose barber shop?"

"My father's," she replied.

"No kiddin'. Guess I didn't mention I'm a barber, too. Second generation. M' dad was a barber."

"Are you serious?"

"No kiddin'."

When the women got out of the car, Carmela looked up at the house and saw her mother standing in the living room window looking down at them (Jack specifically) with a grave expression on her face. As Jack held the door for her, he followed her gaze up to the picture window. He smiled and touched his hat brim, quickly averting his eyes back to Carmela. Raul was holding the back door for Gloria.

It was late in the afternoon. The girls said goodbye to the boys, and Gloria climbed the stairs with Carmela. After they got into the house, they continued their visit in Carmela's room. Teresa didn't want to ask Carmela any questions about the two young men until after Gloria went home. In the meantime she was grumpy and groused around the house.

"How come you're all agüitado?" Carlos finally asked when she flared up at him because he hadn't taken the kitchen trash out.

Teresa didn't answer. She wasn't going to tell him what was eating her till Gloria left. It was a half hour before sunset. Carlos took the kitchen trash out, and when he came back in, Gloria was leaving. Carmela walked with her halfway home.

"Diden't you see those two boys that dropped them off?" Teresa asked Carlos after the girls had left.

"Uh, uh. What about 'em?"

"Well, your daughter got out of the front seat of a junky old car. The driver was a gringo. The boy in the back seat with Gloria looked like a nice Mexicano boy."

"So, what's the problem? She's old enough to be going out with boys."

"I'm not bothered that she was out with a boy. It's just that the boy she was with isn't

35

Mexican. And you know, he's probably not a Catholic, too."

"I still don't see what you're worried about. Ain't like she's go'n'a marry the guy, is it? Híjola! What if she don't never see him again?"

"That's possible, but I think we should have a talk with her anyway. I don't like her mixeen with the gringos."

"Now, Teresa, you're jumping to conclusions?"

Just as Carlos finished saying this, Carmela came in the front door and both of them fell silent. She went to the kitchen and poured herself a glass of milk, and when she came back into the living room, she was aware of the silence and the penetration of her mother's stare.

"So, who were the boys that brought you home this afternoon?" Teresa asked her daughter.

"Oh just a couple of boys we met at Van de Kamp's. They took us down to Olvera Street and the Placita. Their names are Jack and Raul, and guess what Papá? Jack is a barber, and so was his father. They're nice boys."

"You know," Teresa said, "I don't think it's such a good idea to be goeen out with gringo

36

boys. Cultures don't mix, just like religions. I bet he's not even a Catholic."

"Mamá, just listen to you. You sound prejudice. We only just met, and I didn't ask him what his religion is. All I can say is we had fun. And you don't have to worry. I probably won't see him again."

"Goodt thing we don't have a phone so he won't be calleen you."

Carmela was starting to lose her patience. Carlos sat quietly, not wanting to get involved. He was more interested that the young man was a barber than that he wasn't a Mexican or a Catholic. He thought of his own meager lot in life and really wasn't enthusiastic for his daughter to hook up with someone whose prospects were equally as dismal. But then he thought that by simply being a barber, the man's prospects didn't have to be limited.

...look at john....he's doing pretty goddamn good....

So really, the more Carlos thought about it, the less concerned he was with the idea of Carmela going out with a barber. And he really didn't care if she went out with Mexicanos or gavachos. He wasn't worried. As Carmela had said, she'd only just met him that afternoon, and

37

she didn't know if she was ever going to see him again.

"Well, I've seen it happen before where some nice Mexican girl or boy gets involved with an Americano, and it just never works out," Teresa said. "Señora Arredondo's oldest son married an Episcopalian girl from Glendale, and within a year, he'd quit going to Mass. Now la señora says they're separated and will probably eventually get divorced. Heaven forbid that something like that should ever happen to you."

"Oh, Mamá, you're over-reacting. I don't know if I'll ever see the man again."

And without giving Teresa a chance to respond, she went off to her room to read. Teresa looked to Carlos for support, but all he did was shrug his shoulders and step out the front door for a breath of fresh air. He watched the trains moving around in the switching yard on the other side of San Fernando Road, and after only a few minutes, he went back inside. Teresa was on the couch knitting. Carlos sat down in his chair opposite and picked up the want ads from the morning *Times* he'd gotten from the Cypress Gateway on their way home from Mass. He looked over the "barbers" ads. Strains of "Ain't it a Shame" drifted faintly through Carmela's closed bedroom door.

Three

Carlos awoke at six o'clock on Tuesday morning and hit the ground running. The enthusiasm he'd been feeling since his busy Friday and Saturday had carried through Sunday when he'd given his shop a good cleaning. By Monday he was chomping at the bit. He couldn't wait for Tuesday and to open the barber shop for what he hoped would be another busy day. When Tuesday finally arrived, the enthusiasm was still there. He was pumped up. He wanted the busy streak to continue.

Carmela was bustling around the house, trying to get out the door to catch the seven-fifteen streetcar to work. Teresa was packing a lunch for her. When she was ready to go, she hugged her parents and was out the door by seven-ten. Carlos moved to the living room window, pushed the curtains back, and watched her cross the street to the safety zone in front of Contreras' store just as the streetcar pulled up.

"You look like you're ready to conquer the worldt," Teresa said.

"I'm feeling better about the shop since last Friday and Saturday. Think I'm go'n'a start making some feria. Maybe if I get busy enough, Carmela can quit her job, and I can pay for her college."

He'd shaved and taken his shower while Carmela was having her breakfast, so now he was ready for his own breakfast. He and Teresa ate in silence, he contemplating a busy day in the barber shop, she wondering what kind of manager would replace Mister Delbert, who'd been absent from the store on Monday. The word around the store was that he was at his new store getting acquainted with his staff. He'd been such a good boss that she was apprehensive about who the new boss would be.

His replacement was to be announced that same day. She would find out that afternoon when she punched in. She was hoping it wouldn't be Terry Snyder, Mister Delbert's assistant manager. She didn't have a good relationship with him. He was just a little too young and too gringuisimo to suit her. She didn't doubt that he was a nice enough young man. She just thought he was too young to be taking orders from. And then there was the whole question of

The Journeyman and the Apprentice

his gavachismo. Mister Delbert was a gavacho, too, but at least he was old enough for her to respect him when he asked her to do something. Terry was already getting into the job and getting comfortable there. He'd been in charge on Monday.

At five to nine Carlos, horn in hand, left the house and went down to the shop. He waved at Contreras who was sweeping the sidewalk in front of his store. Then, as he'd done every Tuesday for the past nine years, he unlocked his front door, flipped the light switch next to it, went to the back of the shop, took the smock off its hook, put it on and turned on the radio. Then he got the broom out and went to sweep his own sidewalk. When he finished, he went back into the shop and admired his handiwork from Sunday.

...big improvement getting those water spots off the mirrors...place looks más brilloso....

He sat down in his barber chair and stared out the window. Fifteen minutes later, he was sitting on his stool in the back blowing his horn. His first customer didn't come in until ten-twenty-five. He was a traveling salesman Carlos knew only as Tom who came in every ten days for a shave and haircut. The shave took longer to do than the haircut and he charged fifty cents less to do it. Shaves were like kids's haircuts; they were harder to do and more time consuming, but he got less money for them.

After Tom left, Carlos sat around for another half hour, and then he crossed the street to visit with Contreras. They talked for forty-five minutes, and no one approached either of their doors. By twelve-thirty they were both ready to close their doors and go do something else when Carlos saw a young man wearing a panama fedora pacing back and forth in front of his shop, looking in the window. He was acting like he wanted to go in, but then he'd hesitate and walk away from the front door, but not leave altogether. After watching this for a minute or two, Carlos decided to go over and see what was on his mind.

"Something I can do for you?"

"You Carlos?"

"Yeah, I'm Carlos," he replied, pointing to the sign on the fascia above the window. "You want a haircut?"

"Naw, I'm a barber. Name's Jack Niel." The young man with the dark hair and blue eyes touched his hat brim with his left hand, offered his right hand, and Carlos took it. "I was j'st

The Journeyman and the Apprentice

wondering if you're lookin' for a barber for your second chair."

Carlos hesitated, taken aback by the suggestion. Just because it was obvious to *him* that business was slow didn't mean it was obvious to anybody else who looked even casually at the situation. It was hard for him to imagine anybody asking such a question.

"You a journeyman?" he finally asked, going inside. Jack followed.

"Had my apprentice license for about six months. I was a Navy barber for three years before I went to school. I graduated from American Barber College. One on Main Street. Been workin' in a shop up on Verdugo ever since. Got four year's experience, total. Plus, my dad was a barber, and I spent a lota' time watchin' him when I was a kid." Carmela's description of the young man she was with Sunday came to Carlos' mind. "Hey, I c'n do a good flat top— too good for the shop where I'm at. Wha'da yuh say? C'n yuh use someone?"

"Well, not really. I barely got enough for myself."

"I got a small following, and I think a lot of 'em'll go wherever I go. I know they'll follow me this close. It's only a mile down the road."

Jerome Arthur

"Navy barber, huh?"

"Yep."

"Me too. But I was already a barber before I went in."

The part about him being good with flat tops was the thing that really got Carlos' attention, and he would have hired him on that alone, but he was still faced with the reality that business was just plain slow. He hardly had enough for himself, and he thought that no matter how good this kid was with flat tops, if nobody was coming through the door looking for them, it was useless to think about hiring *anybody*. He sat down in his chair, and Jack sat opposite him in one of the waiting chairs.

"Just ain't enough business here for two barbers," he finally said.

"Hey, I understand, but if you hire me, there'll be business. I'll bring some with me, and then I'll go out and hustle some new customers, too. I grew up right over here in Eagle Rock and Highland Park. A lota' the guys I grew up with still live there. Ain't that far away, so they'll prob'ly be comin' down. What yuh got to lose? I'll work on straight commission. Seventy percent. If I don't cut no hair, I don't make no money. Nothin' comes outa' *your* pocket."

44

The Journeyman and the Apprentice

Visions of the post war years came into Carlos' head, when he and Jonesy were so busy that sometimes he'd lose a dollar or two under the cash drawer and not discover it for a week or two and not miss it in the meantime. But he was still skeptical no matter how such visions played on his mind.

...kid's got a good line...good personality, too...bet he could do it...talks like a mexicano, but i know he ain't one...too light-complected...i ought'a put him to work just to see if he can deliver the goods like he says....

"If I give yuh the job, how soon yuh be able to come to work?"

"I c'n give my boss a week's notice soon's I get back from lunch. Could be on the job next Tuesday. That soon enough?"

"Okay, you got the second chair, but I'm warnin' yuh, I ain't doin' no land office business here."

Jack reacted to this as though Carlos had just told him that he was going to be busier than he'd ever been in his life. He got even more animated than he'd been for the last ten minutes. He took Carlos' hand and pumped it enthusiastically.

"Yuh ain't go'n'a be sorry, eh. We're both go'n'a be busy. You'll see."

"Okay. You go give your boss notice and be in touch with me before you come in next Tuesday."

"Órale, Carlos. Be talking to you soon. Right now I got'a get back. Lunch hour's almost over."

Carlos did a double take on that one. The kid spoke chicano Spanish. He followed him out the door and stood in the doorway watching him walk to the next block and get into his beat up old 'thirty-nine Chevy and drive off.

...the hell've i gone and done now?...only done one shave and one haircut all day, and i went and hired a damn barber for the second chair....

As Jack drove off, Teresa came down the stairs and left for work.

"Guess I'll find out who my new boss is today," she said as she kissed Carlos goodbye.

"Good luck," he said.

She hugged him and walked off down the street. After he had lunch, Carlos went back across the street to Contreras' store, but only for a minute. A customer walked up to his front door just as he was going into the grocery store. He turned and went back across the street. That was the start of a run of three haircuts at the end of which there was an hour hiatus. At that point

46

The Journeyman and the Apprentice

Carlos crossed the street and read the Eight Star with Enrique. He finished reading just in time to do the last two haircuts of the day.

Carlos was the first to enter the house at six o'clock. Teresa showed up for her dinner break ten minutes later. Carmela had class that night and wouldn't be home until a quarter to eleven. Teresa wasn't talking as she prepared their dinner. A shadow hung over her, and for all Carlos knew one was hanging over him, too. He'd cut all of eight-dollars-and-a-quarter-worth of hair that day.

Teresa didn't start talking until they were eating dinner. With the strains of big band music on the radio as background, Carlos listened as Teresa told him that Terry Snyder was going to be her new manager. When they finished eating, she left to go back to work, and Carlos went down the stairs with her and crossed the street to Contreras' store. Since nobody was home, he hung around with Enrique as he closed up for the night.

Alone in the house, he sat and played his sax and thought about his new employee. He had mixed feelings about it. On the one hand, he worried that Jack would come into his shop and sit around and not cut any hair. Then on the other hand, it wasn't going to cost him a cent to

Jerome Arthur

have the kid there, so he quit worrying about it
and thought about the possibility that the kid
might improve business as he'd said.

At nine-thirty Carlos took off to meet
Teresa at the end of her shift. A streetcar came
over the rise when they got to Cypress Avenue,
so they stepped out onto the safety zone as it
approached. It turned out to be the coldest night
of the season, and the warm streetcar was a nice
relief. When they got home, he turned the radio
on, and they listened to Duke Ellington as they
waited for Carmela to come home. She'd be on
the next streetcar. Teresa knitted and they
talked. Since the shop was so slow that day, he
thought better of telling her that he'd hired a
barber. She'd only question the good sense of
such a move, and he had to admit that the question would be justified.

*...why didn't i think of any of this before
i gave the kid the job?...maybe it won't matter
when she meets him and hears him talk....*

Carmela got home at a quarter to eleven
and went straight to bed. Carlos turned the radio
off, and Teresa put her knitting things away.
The two of them went off to their bedroom.

*   *   *

48

The Journeyman and the Apprentice

At five after one, Jack got back to the shop where he worked, and his boss looked at him askance, but he paid no attention. He went to the back room and put on his smock. When he got back out front, he sat in one of the waiting chairs and watched as the boss and the barber in the second chair worked on haircuts. The barber in the third chair was still at lunch, and the barber in the fourth chair had gone to lunch when Jack came back. He picked up a *Time* magazine from the stack on the table and thumbed through it. Bored, he set the magazine down, got up, walked out to the front of the shop and stood on the sidewalk by the front door.

...go'n'a be easier to build up a clientele at carlos' shop...too many barbers here...pinchi pendejo j.b. the second chair keeps takin' customers outa' turn...lucky i'm doin' anything, way he jumps' up and grabs everything comes through the door...el matador with the haircloth....

As these thoughts coursed through his head, a customer approached, and Jack followed him in the door, asking him if he'd like to be next, but he sat down opposite J.B.'s chair and said he'd wait for him. Jack went back out to the sidewalk and watched the traffic.

Jerome Arthur

...ain't no use goin' out and tryin' to hustle new customers...ain't go'n'a be here next week...save the hustlin' for carlos' shop....

The barber in the third chair came back from lunch followed in the door by one of his regulars. The boss finished doing the haircut he was working on and swept the floor. When he finished that chore, he went out front and stood next to Jack.

"Yuh know," he said, "yuh can't be coming back from lunch late all the time. It screws up the other guys's lunch hours. I know you're not too busy right now, but yuh got'a keep regular hours if yuh wan'a *get* busy."

"Know what? I'm quitin' enda' the week. Found me another job. Boss there wants me to start on Tuesday. To be honest, I don't think I'm ever go'n'a make it here, buried back there in the fifth chair and J.B. takin' every customer comes through the door...."

He trailed off and waited for a response, but none came. They both stood there in silence for a minute or two. Jack's heart was pounding. He couldn't believe how nervous he was.

"Well, I don't know what yuh mean about J.B. taking all the customers," the boss finally said. "He's got his regulars, and I don't know anything about him takin' customers from

50

The Journeyman and the Apprentice

the other barbers. Maybe yuh ought'a just move on to your new job right away. I mean," a shrug, "what's the point hangin' around here for another week if you're not go'n'a be here after that? Why don't yuh finish up today. I'll pay yuh off tonight, and you can move on."

"Yeah, guess that's what I ought'a do. 'Am kinda' anxious to get started in my new gig."

Just then a customer who usually didn't wait for any barber in particular came to the front door. The boss escorted him into the shop and seated him in his own chair. Jack watched this in open-mouthed astonishment.

...i can't believe he just did that....

He walked straight back to his own chair, got out his bag and started packing his tools. When the boss saw what he was doing, he went back to Jack's chair.

"The hell're yuh doin'?"

He asked this quietly, his back to the three occupied chairs in the front part of the shop.

"I'm outa' here. You just pulled a J.B. on me. I been hangin' around watchin' you guys doin' all the haircuts. No more."

He said this as he packed his bag. They were both keeping their voices down. The other

51

barbers and customers couldn't hear them. Jack's heart was racing, and he was on the verge of exploding into a rant on the virtues of the "turn system."

"I'll come back at closing time to pick up my pay for the three cuts I did this morning."

He knew if he stuck around and took care of it right then, he wouldn't be keeping his voice down, and he'd make a scene. The boss went to his own chair and got back to work. Jack made one quick scan of his workstation to make sure he hadn't left anything behind, and then he picked up his bag of tools and headed out the door.

When he got to his car, he stopped and thought for a minute about what he'd do next. He decided to go someplace, get an ice-cold beer and relax. He drove up a few blocks to the As Is, a little dive on Verdugo near Fletcher Drive. It was dark and cool and quiet inside. He was the only person in the joint. It wasn't even two o'clock. The bartender moved around behind the bar, washing glasses, and starting up a pot of coffee. As Jack sat drinking his beer, one of the regulars came in out of the bright sunshine and sat down on a barstool at the other end of the bar.

The Journeyman and the Apprentice

"Hey, Antoine, how you doin'?" asked the bartender.

"Pretty good, Joe. How 'bout you?"

"Okay. Just got a lot to do here is all. Damn night man left the place a mess. What'll yuh have?"

"Shot a' Jack Daniels and a backer."

"Comin' up."

The bartender set a shot glass in front of him and filled it to the brim from a fifth bottle of Jack Daniels. Then he drew a draft from the tap and set it down next to the whiskey.

"Here's mud in your eye," Antoine said knocking back the whiskey and washing it down with a big swig of beer. Then tapping the empty shot glass on the bar, he said, "Do it again."

The bartender filled the shot glass.

"You go'n'a go to work today?" he asked setting the fifth bottle back in the well behind the bar.

"Yeah. Got about an hour and a half. This is the only way I c'n face it. Damn swing shift plays hell with a guy's night life. Yuh got'a do it during the day."

With a sidelong glance so as not to appear to be staring, Jack could see that the customer was sipping the second shot. He couldn't believe the guy could be drinking so heavily be-

Jerome Arthur

fore going to work. He wondered what kind of a job the guy had. Then he finished his own beer, got down off his barstool and headed for the door.

"Thanks a lot," the bartender said as he passed behind Antoine on his way out.

"Sure," Jack said. "See yuh later."

Stepping out into the sunlight from the dark barroom, he was temporarily blinded. It took his eyes a minute to adjust. He thought about what to do with the rest of his day.

...wonder if i should just go down carlos' place, see if he wants me to go 'head on, set up my tools...or maybe go over see what raul's doin'...he's off today....

"How come yuh ain't workin'?" Raul asked when he answered the door. "I was just go'n'a go over your shop, hang out for a while, shoot the shit."

"I quit, eh. Got me another job. Goin' to work in that shop over Cypress. The father a' that chavala we met over Van de Kamp's day before yesterday? Only problem is, he don't want me till next week, eh. I already quit the other jale."

"You been a busy vato, eh. I can't believe all this happened already, man."

54

The Journeyman and the Apprentice

"Yeah, well I'm really go'n'a have to hustle for my bread now. Had to talk the vato into hiring me. Tol' me he ain't even got enough for himself, eh."

"So, wha'da yuh wan'a go into a deal like that for? How yuh go'n'a make any feria?"

"Just go'n'a have to hustle."

"Yeah, I guess if anybody c'n hustle haircuts, it's you."

"Yuh know where I'm go'n'a start? In that bar down San Fernando across from the train yard. Place packs 'em in every day. Lota' workin' guys, carpenters, railroad workers, electricians. Yuh wan'a take a ride down there and look it over? Feel like an ice-cold beer?"

"Órale, ese, let's go 'head on. Cold beer sounds good."

There were two guys sitting at opposite ends of the bar when they walked in. The bartender leaned against one of the wood framed glass doors of a big cooler and stared straight ahead, not talking to either of the two guys. Jack and Raul took two barstools in front of where the bartender was standing.

"What'll you have, gents?" he asked.

"Couple a' drafts," Jack replied.

The bartender took two frosty mugs out of a cold box behind him and filled them with

Jerome Arthur

Eastside from one of the taps. After he put the money in the cash register, he returned to his position in front of the cooler. He didn't say a word. It was going to be up to Jack to start a conversation.

"Guess we're early enough to beat the rush, huh?" he said.

"Wha'da yuh mean?" asked the bartender.

"Seems like every time I drive by here later in the afternoon, there's a big crowd spilling out the front door."

"Yeah, well, it's usually slow this time a' day," said the bartender. "Guys get off around five, six o'clock. Gets busy then."

"Every day?"

"Yeah. Weekdays are the busiest. Saturday gets busy at night. We're closed Sundays."

"Yeah, well, I guess you'll be seein' more a' me from now on. Go'n'a be working in Carlos' Barber Shop right up the street here on Cypress."

"No kiddin'. I used to get my hair cut from Jonesy. Now, I go to Bob at John's shop. He gives me a real good flat top with long sides. Yuh c'n see how it looks. Pretty good, huh?"

The Journeyman and the Apprentice

"Yeah, it's not bad. Check out Raul's flat top, here. That's the kinda' work I do. Yuh ought'a give me a try next time."

"Yeah, maybe I will."

He went up front to the end of the bar and filled a customer's empty mug. He stayed and talked to the guy for a little while, periodically looking down the length of the bar to see how Jack and Raul and the other guy were doing. The guy at the other end emptied his glass and got up and moved toward the door. Looking like a silhouetted ghost, he was framed by the rectangle of light that flooded the bar from the open door. As he stepped out and closed the door behind him, the bar got dark again, the only light being the shaded incandescents enshrouded in cobwebs behind the bar. Jack and Raul drained their glasses, prompting the bartender to approach them for refills, but they were off their stools before he could get to them.

"Come see me at Carlos' shop next time you need a haircut," Jack said.

"See you guys later."

Then it was their turn to be silhouettes as they stepped into the glowing oblong of the open front door.

"Think I'm go'n'a drop in on Carlos to-morrow. Hope it'll be okay. Alls he can do is tell me to come back next Tuesday."

"I'll come by during my lunch hour for a haircut. I could use one, and he'd have to let you work, wouldn't he?"

"Yeah, I guess so, but I might not be there if he tells me to go home and come back Tuesday."

"Wouldn't it look good if I came by and asked for yuh?"

"Definitely."

They drove up to Cypress and cruised slowly past the shop. Carlos was letting a customer out of the chair, and another one was getting out of his car and going for the front door.

"Don't look that slow to me," Raul said. "Look at that, two haircuts in a row."

"Yeah, but you ain't been here for the rest of the day. Those two might be the only ones he's done all day. Let's cruise by John's shop. See how he's doing."

Jack turned onto a side street and turned the car around in a driveway. As he passed, he slowed down enough to see that John and Bob were both working on haircuts and there were three people occupying the waiting chairs. He got turned around again and drove back to

58

The Journeyman and the Apprentice

Raul's house where the two of them spent the rest of the afternoon hanging around on the front porch. Nobody else was home so they had the place to themselves. It was like one of those high school afternoons when there was nothing to do, no place to be, just hang around with a buddy and wait for his parents to come home.

Raul's brother Eddie came home from varsity football practice at five o'clock and hung around with them. The afternoon was moving on toward evening and their parents would be home soon. Jack started thinking about going home. He felt pretty lucky to have his own place, but sometimes it got lonely, and when he saw how Raul had his parents and brother to keep him company, he envied him.

"Think I'm go'n'a go get my money from my ex-boss, and then go on home. Maybe I'll see yuh tomorrow, huh?"

"Yeah," Raul said. "If he let's you work, look for me at a little after noon."

"Okay, see yuh later."

He drove up to the shop, and his ex-boss had his money all ready for him, so he picked it up and got out of there without an argument. Then he went home. He turned on the radio and looked in the cupboard for something to eat. He found a can of chili which he dumped into a saucepan and put on the stove to heat up. When he finished eating, he looked for something to wear for tomorrow and realized he didn't have any clean clothes, so he filled his laundry bag and drove up to Highland Park to the laundromat on Figueroa. By the time he got his clean clothes put away, it was getting close to ten o'clock, so he washed his face, brushed his teeth and got into bed.

A few days ago, he came across a book called *Cannery Row*, and he noticed that it was written by John Steinbeck, the same author as a book he'd gotten from the ship's library. That book was *Tortilla Flat*. He'd liked it a lot, and when he'd seen this one by the same author, he bought it. He lay in bed and started to read. He'd never really been much of a reader, but of late he was taking more of an interest in it. He didn't get far that night. It was late and he'd had a lot going on that day and now he was sleepy, so it wasn't long before his eyes drooped and his head nodded. He folded over the corner of the page he was on and dropped the book onto the floor next to the bed. He turned off the light and fell asleep.

Four

At nine o'clock sharp Jack approached the front door of Carlos' Barber Shop. He left his tools in the car. He could get them quickly if he had to. He thought it would be better to go in and talk to Carlos first, see if he even wanted him to show up today.

Carlos had come in early and was cleaning up around the second chair workstation. He'd brought the Electrolux down from the house and was going through the cabinet drawers and compartments with it. He found a box of business cards he'd remembered having printed when Jonesy was still working for him.

...damn seal on the box ain't even broke...whatever it cost me to have 'em printed was a waste of moneda....

He found a half-empty bottle of Stephan's non-alcoholic hair tonic and an empty Lan

Lay bottle. He was vacuuming out a drawer when Jack entered.

"Hey, you came early. Didn't think I'd see you till Tuesday."

"C'n I start now? Gave notice and my ex-boss told me to go 'head on and hit the road. So here I am."

"Just started cleaning up your work-station, eh. It ain't ready yet."

"Here, I c'n do it. I ain't got nothin' else goin' on."

Jack pulled out another drawer and took the vacuum hose out of Carlos' hand. It took about forty-five minutes to get everything cleared out of the cabinet and to wash down the area with some ammonia water and a hand towel. Carlos put all the stuff in a cardboard box and stored it in the enclosed alcove at the rear of the shop. The business cards were still sitting on the narrow counter just above the shampoo bowl between the two cabinets.

"Guess I should get my tools and get set up, huh?" Jack said.

"Hey, why not? You been here for almost an hour, and this is about as busy as it gets, but, yeah, go get your tools."

Jack had parked his car on the side street down behind Contreras' market. He left the

The Journeyman and the Apprentice

shop and crossed the street in that direction. When he got back, Carlos had just started on a haircut. As he unpacked his bag, he noticed the box of business cards Carlos had left on the narrow shelf that connected the two backbars. A card was taped to the end of the box facing him. It was white with plain black print, and all it said was CARLOS' BARBER SHOP in bold print at the center. The address and phone number of the pay phone on the opposite wall next to the cash register were printed along the bottom in smaller type. In the upper left-hand corner was a barber pole.

"Hey, Carlos, could I take a few of these to pass out."

"Sure. Been there for years, and you can see how many I used."

After Jack got his tools set up, he broke the seals on the box. He took about twenty-five cards out and printed his own name neatly in the upper right-hand corner. It was now almost ten-thirty. He stood on the sidewalk next to the front door and looked down Cypress past John's shop at the Gateway store. He poked his head in the door and told Carlos he was going there, and he'd be back in a few minutes. John's shop was just as busy as it had been yesterday. John and Bob both had customers in their chairs, and a couple waiting. In the grocery store, he got a Baby Ruth, and as he paid for it, he handed the checker a card.

"Just started workin' there today," he said, pointing at the card. "Come on down and give me a try. I'll give you a good flat top."

"Really?" the checker asked, surprised. "Isn't mine that good?"

"It's okay, but I'll give you a better one, and I ain't kiddin'."

"Hm. Maybe I'll check it out."

He took out his wallet, put the card in it, and slipped it back into his hip pocket.

Just then, a box boy came up to the end of the check stand and prepared to bag the groceries of the next person in line. Jack took out another card and offered it to him. He gave him the same line he gave the checker, except he substituted haircut for flat top since the box boy had a regular haircut, square cut at the neckline with a duck tail. He got rid of five more cards at some of the other businesses along the avenue. He'd simply walk in, introduce himself, and then offer one of his cards to the person he was talking to.

When Jack got back to the shop, Carlos was sitting in his chair staring out the front win-

The Journeyman and the Apprentice

dow. Jack sat down in the waiting chair opposite.

"You grow up in this neighborhood?" he asked Carlos.

"Uh, uh. Hazard over by the hospital. Went to school at Santa Teresita. Me and my wife been together since eighth grade."

"No kiddin'. Long time."

"Got married soon's she turned twenty-one."

"How'd yuh get into barbering?"

"Went to barber college soon's I graduated high school?"

"And how'd yuh get to Cypress from Hazard."

"I was just back from the war, and this whole piece of property came on the market, so I bought it and brought my family over here. How about you? Where'd you say you grew up?"

"Eagle Rock. I didn't graduate from high school. Went in the Navy when I was a senior. Did a kiddie cruise. Got out day before I turned twenty-one."

It was coming up on lunch time, so Jack took a walk down to San Fernando Road to the saloon he and Raul had gone to yesterday. The same guy was tending bar. Jack squeezed between two barstools and leaned on the bar. He took a card from his wallet and put it down in front of the bartender.

"'Member me from yesterday?" he said. "I'm officially workin' for Carlos now. Here's my card."

"All right! Wan'a beer?"

"Naw, it's too early. Plus, I got'a get back so Carlos can go to lunch. I'll be back later on."

When he got back, the shop was busy. Carlos had a customer in the chair, and there was a kid waiting. Raul was there too. Jack had forgotten that he'd said he'd be in for a cut at lunchtime.

"You get here before him?" Jack asked Raul as he nodded toward the kid.

"No, he was here first, so go 'head on and take him. I c'n wait."

"Sure. That'd be cool."

Jack told the kid to get in his chair. The guy in Carlos' chair spoke up.

"Yeah, he wants a flat top. Carlos'll tell yuh how."

So as Jack got the kid into his chair, Carlos turned to him and told him to make it close on the sides and flat on top.

The Journeyman and the Apprentice

By the end of the day Jack had done four haircuts and Carlos six. Raul got into Jack's chair at twelve-twenty after he finished the kid with the flat top, and at one o'clock the checker from Gateway came in and got a flat top. Carlos wasn't busy just then, so he watched Jack do the job. He was impressed.

...he wasn't lying when he said he did a good flat top...did a great job on joe's kid this morning....

At a quarter to two Teresa came to the front door, and Carlos tried to intercept her before she came in, but he wasn't quick enough.

"I'm goeen to work, mi querido..." she said and stopped dead in her tracks when she saw Jack sitting on a stool pulled up to his backbar, honing a razor.

"Oh," Carlos stammered. "This is Jack, honey. Just started working here this morning."

"Hello," Jack said, standing up from his stool, putting down the hone and razor and tipping his hat.

He wore a big smile, but he somehow sensed that he shouldn't offer his hand, and that was a good thing, because Teresa wouldn't have taken it. As it was, she didn't respond to him verbally. She didn't even bow her head. She acknowledged his presence by staring as she

67

took Carlos by the hand and walked him out the front door and around the corner of the shop.

"I guess we'll have to talk about this later when I get home from work," she said. "Meanwhile, I still love you."

She hugged him and headed off down the street toward Figueroa, looking straight ahead as she passed the front window of the shop, not even turning slightly, lest she see Jack out of the corner of her eye. He, on the other hand, was staring intently out the same window to get as much of a look at her as he could. Carlos went back into the shop.

At a quarter to six when Carmela passed by the front window and saw Jack cutting hair alongside her father, she couldn't believe her eyes. Since Carlos had his back to the window, he didn't see her until she opened the door, and then he spotted her in the mirror on the back wall.

"Hi, Papá. Hello, Jack."

"Hi, Carmela."

"What are you doing here?"

"Workin'. Just started today. Workin' out pretty good too, huh, Carlos?"

"So far, so good. You two know each other?"

The Journeyman and the Apprentice

"He's the boy I was with on Sunday. We met at Van de Kamp's."

"Oooh," Carlos said, as though something were just then dawning on him.

...now i get it...jack's the guy teresa was so upset about when the girls came home sunday....

But in fact Teresa didn't recognize him at first because when she saw him holding the open car door for Carmela, his trademark Panama, with its two-and-a-half-inch brim, half hid his face. She'd only gotten a momentary glimpse of him when he'd followed Carmela's gaze up to the picture window she was standing in. All she saw when she walked into the shop was another barber honing his razor and waiting for a customer to walk through the door. It was when she saw the hat, that it dawned on her who he was.

"And he's a gringo, too," she would later say to Carlos at the dinner table. "You know this neighborhoodt is full of Mexicanos. How will he ever get any of them into his chair? What couldt you have been thinkeen when you hiredt him, mi esposo querido?"

Carmela only stayed for a minute or two. The two barbers were busy, and she had to get upstairs to start dinner. Jack finished his cut be-

Jerome Arthur

fore Carlos, so Carlos sent him across the street to Contreras' store to pick up a couple bottles of Eastside.

"Not a bad day," said Carlos as they cleaned up their workstations and swept the floor, "but we got'a do better, eh. It kinda' caught me off guard when those two guys came in and asked for you. That was good."

"Yeah, well, I'm even go'n'a have more people coming in and asking for me. You'll see."

When they were finished, Carlos went up the stairs, and Jack walked down to San Fernando to the bar and had another beer. It was packed, but he could see that the crowd was thinning out. It had been much busier an hour earlier. He found a vacant barstool and sat down, immediately striking up a conversation with the guy on the next stool, and before long he was giving him his card. The guy lived in Glassell Park and worked downtown. He stopped by the bar a couple times a week on his way home. He told Jack he'd try to get in to see him, and then he ordered another beer. Jack finished his, walked back to his car and went home.

*   *   *

70

The Journeyman and the Apprentice

"How can you possibly hire a barber when you barely got enough business for your-salf?" Teresa asked Carlos. "And I can't believe you didt this without sayeen a word to me. He obviously didn't just walk in off the street to-day. You must've known about this before to-day. Why didn't you say sometheen about it?"

"I only knew about it since yesterday, and he wasn't even supposed to come in till next Tuesday. I was go'n'a tell you before then, but he showed up this morning. It ain't go'n'a cost me nothing. He's go'n'a bring his own custom-ers in, and he's working for straight seventy percent, so if he don't cut no hair, he ain't go'n'a make no dough. I don't got'a pay him a cent."

"But suppose he doesn't bring in any new customers. He'll take customers away from *you*."

"Don't think so, honey. He already brought in two new ones today. You should see the flat tops he does. Shop's go'n'a be busy again."

Carmela ate dinner and didn't say a word to interrupt them. She hadn't heard her parents in such a lively debate in a long time. The way the conversation was going, she could tell that her mother still wasn't getting it that Jack was the same boy who'd dropped her off on Sunday afternoon, and she didn't say or do anything to remind Teresa of it. She remembered her reaction to him then, and she didn't want to stir those feelings up again. And besides, as far as Carmela was concerned, there really wasn't anything between her and Jack, so what was the use of rousing her mother's bad feelings again?

"Mexicanos in this neighborhoodt won't let him cut their hair."

"I wouldn't say that," Carlos responded. "He speaks a little Spanish, and you ought'a hear how good. Couple ones he did today were Mexicans."

Carlos hadn't actually heard him speak any Spanish, except for "vato" and "órale," but the accent was right for those colloquialisms, so Carlos assumed Jack could speak some Spanish.

"That don't make no difference. They'll take one look at that blond hair, and he won't get a chance to show what kind of Spanish he can speak, if, as you say, he speaks any Spanish at all."

"His hair's as black as yours, Mamá," Carmela finally said. "And besides, not every-

The Journeyman and the Apprentice

body looks at skin and hair color the same way you do."

"¡Cállate!" Teresa said sharply. "What do you think this is about? It's about you, and whether we have enough money to ever send you to college. If this young man doesn't work out in your father's shop, it couldt be a setback to your college education. And besides, how do you know what color his hair is?"

Carmela made no response to this. Teresa was so completely in charge here that Carlos was also silenced. She was on a roll, and there was nothing either of them could say or do to stop her. But her last question suddenly made her aware of who Jack was.

"Oh, no! He's the boy you were with last Sunday, isn't he?" she said to Carmela, and now to Carlos, "I know it's your shop and your business, but how you run it affects us all, so I think you shouldt tal' the young man that he can't work for you no more."

"Sorry, baby, but I can't do that. 'Sides, I think he's go'n'a be good for the shop, and I ought'a at least give him a chance to prove it. I hear what you're saying, but I should try it out for at least a month, and if it don't work out, I can always let 'im go later."

Jerome Arthur

That ended the conversation. They ate the rest of the meal in silence. After dinner, instead of listening to the radio, Carlos went back down to the shop and spent about a half hour straightening up, getting ready for the morning.

*   *   *

As for Jack, when he left the bar, he went home and killed off the half can of chili con carne in the refrigerator. After he ate, he spent the rest of the evening lying on his bed reading *Cannery Row*. He was so excited about his prospects on his new job that he had trouble concentrating on the story. Eventually, he laid the book face-down on his chest, stared at the wall opposite and thought about Carmela and her mother. He didn't know quite how to take Teresa. He was determined to be courteous, but he had the distinct feeling that she didn't like him. Then he thought about the shop and the good feeling he got from his first day on the job, which he needed to do because Thursday and Friday were disappointments by comparison, but on Saturday Carlos did ten cuts and Jack did six.

He'd only caught glimpses of Teresa during the rest of the week, and all he saw of

74

The Journeyman and the Apprentice

Carmela was when she passed by the front window at a quarter to six and stuck her head in the door. He thought about her quite a bit. He was mostly trying to figure out some way to approach her, ask her if she'd like to go out sometime. After greeting Carlos, she seemed to quicken her pace around the corner and up the stairs. Jack began to think she was trying to avoid him. Then remembering the icy reception he'd received from Teresa the other day and her subsequent scarce appearance, he thought that perhaps Carmela was being steered away from him by her mother. But none of that prevented him from always putting on a smiling face every time Carmela passed by.

...i'll kill her with kindness...keep smiling and she'll loosen up...same with her mother....

When she didn't pass by the front window on Saturday afternoon, which only made sense since she didn't work Saturdays, he found that he actually missed her. He thought she must have gone out earlier in the day, probably when he was doing a haircut. He didn't have a late haircut, so he went out on the sidewalk and stood around watching for her, hoping she'd make an appearance before his day ended. He waited in vain, and at five to five he went to

Contreras' store and picked up a couple of Eastsides. He looked straight up at the house as he crossed the street back to the shop, but no one appeared in the window.

Carmela actually had passed by the front window earlier in the day. It was just as Jack had thought. He was busy cutting hair and didn't see her. She went to Gloria's house. They had gone to the theater district downtown and seen a matinee showing of *On the Waterfront* at the Orpheum. They were both big Brando fans; they'd seen every picture he'd been in. After the movie they hung around downtown for a couple of hours, going in and out of the department stores on Broadway. They didn't spend any money, but they took things off racks and held them up to their bodies and admired themselves in the tall department store mirrors.

Then they went to Clifton's South Seas Cafeteria on Olive for dinner. When they finished eating, they went back to Broadway and caught the Five Eagle Rock to Cypress Park. It was dark when they got home, and the October evening was getting cool. They hadn't taken sweaters when they left in the afternoon, and by the time they got home, they wished they'd had them. It was warm inside the streetcar, but while waiting for it, the two women were feeling the

The Journeyman and the Apprentice

chill. It was past seven o'clock when Carmela scurried up the steps.

A quiet hung over the house when she entered. It was the silence of a cease fire, not the surrender of a white flag. The battle would be fought off and on till Thanksgiving. If Jack was still working the second chair by then, Teresa would go back on the war path. If he wasn't, Carlos would be down in the dumps again. He was finding that he liked having Jack around, even when the business was slow. Either way if the truce ended, there would be domestic warfare once again. Teresa couldn't bring herself to admit she was wrong about Jack, no matter how successful and busy he got, and she would continue to try to convince Carlos to get rid of him.

Carmela was secretly rooting for Jack, hoping that his success would silence her mother's prejudice. Also, she liked him and wanted to see him do well, which in turn would bring prosperity to her father, and she wanted that more than anything. It would get her into college sooner, but mostly her father would be happy because his shop would be busy and he'd be making money.

Five

On Sunday morning Carlos, Teresa and Carmela set out for Mass, and on the way, they stopped again at Señora Guevara's house. Carmela had left early to walk the two blocks past the church to Gloria's house. The two young women had agreed the day before at the movie that Gloria would join the Rángels. By the time they got to the church, the family had already gone in. To the young women's surprise, Jack and Raul came up the sidewalk as they climbed the church steps.

"Hi, how yuh doin'?" Jack said to Carmela.

"I'm fine. How are you? I'm surprised to see you here?"

"Hopin' we'd run into yuh. C'n we join yuh at Mass?"

"We can't stop you," Carmela replied.

The Journeyman and the Apprentice

"Of course you can accompany us in," Gloria said, "and we better get goeen or we'll be late."

And with that they entered the church. The priest and the altar boys were just coming out of the sacristy as they took their seats in the pew next to Carlos, Teresa and Señora Guevara. Teresa was not happy to see the two young men with Carmela and Gloria.

Everybody in the group except Carlos and Jack received holy communion, the former because he hadn't gone to confession, the latter because he'd quit observing Catholic rituals long ago. This was the first time he'd been to Mass since boot camp. Oh, he'd gone a couple times since then with David Pacheco, his best friend in the Navy, but he didn't go to communion, and he wasn't really worshipping on either of those occasions. He just showed up for David's mother's benefit. Teresa took special notice of the fact that he didn't receive communion.

...just as i thought...he's not a catholic....

On the sidewalk after Mass, Gloria stayed close to Raul and talked to him. It was only by happenstance that Carmela ended up standing next to Jack, but they were soon sepa-

Jerome Arthur

rated as Teresa was suddenly in a hurry to be getting home. Before the young people were split up, however, they'd managed to arrange a meeting at Van de Kamp's for one o'clock. This was mainly Gloria's doing. Indeed, she wanted to get together with Raul, but she also wanted it to be a double date with Jack and Carmela. Carmela was the only one of the four who wasn't eager to go, but she agreed to it to please Gloria.

They split up at the church. Jack and Raul drove over to the east side to see David Pacheco. He hadn't seen him or his parents in quite a while. From the start they'd taken Jack in and treated him like family, and since his parents had died in an automobile accident when he was in boot camp, and he therefore no longer had parents of his own, he took to it and accepted the Pachecos as his parents. He was right at home with the family.

*   *   *

When he was sixteen, Jack had hotwired a car and got busted for joyriding. That earned him a stint at the Optimist Home for Boys on Figueroa. It was a school for delinquents run by the Optimist Club of Eagle Rock. He was re-

80

The Journeyman and the Apprentice

leased a year later and sent back to his parents, and three months after his release, he got caught hotwiring another car. The judge in that case gave him two options. Since he was now seventeen, old enough for military service, that was one of his choices. The other was to be sent to the Pacific Lodge Boy's Home in San Fernando Valley. At that rate, he was well on his way to Preston, a California Youth Authority facility in the San Joaquín Valley.

He chose the Navy and enlisted for a "kiddie cruise." He would be released from active service a day before his twenty-first birthday. In boot camp he decided to follow in his father's footsteps. He struck for Ship Serviceman and became a Navy barber. In one of his last acts, his dad had given him a set of haircutting tools (a Wahl electric clipper, a pair of shears and a comb) as he was leaving for boot camp in San Diego. He started immediately cutting his fellow recruits' hair. They had to pay the barbers at the Navy exchange, who were civil service workers and not real barbers, a quarter for their haircuts, and it was a requirement to get one once a week. Jack would charge them a dime, and he'd sometimes make as much as two dollars the two days before dress inspection. He was even cutting the company commander's hair who wasn't a recruit, but a first-class boatswain's mate.

By the time he got his first assignment on board the aircraft carrier U.S.S. Kearsarge, he had a pretty good feel for the haircutting tools, and for the heads he was working on. Indeed, he'd had plenty of experience observing his dad cutting hair as he was growing up, so he knew a little something about it going in. He met David Pacheco in boot camp and when they got out of basic, they struck for the same rate, and both got stationed on the Kearsarge. David worked as a clerk in the ship's exchange which was right next to the barber shop. He and Jack became fast friends, like brothers, which the Pachecos saw the first time Jack came home to the Fourth Flats neighborhood of east Los Angeles with David. That was when he started learning Spanish.

*   *   *

On that Sunday, Jack and Raul visited with the Pachecos for an hour and a half. David wasn't there because he was bagging groceries at Ralph's over on Beverly Boulevard. Señora Pacheco heated up a pot of beans and some tortillas. They ate while they talked, bringing each

The Journeyman and the Apprentice

other up to date on what they were doing. Jack told them about his recent job change.

He and Raul got on the road to Van de Kamp's by noon. At the restaurant he found an empty space in the drive-in, so he took it. It was ten to one, and the girls weren't there yet. When the car hop came up, Jack and Raul ordered Cokes, and told her they'd order lunch when the girls got there. Soon after the waitress skated off, the two young women showed up. Raul got out of the car as they approached, and he held the doors for them. Carmela got into the front with Jack, and Raul followed Gloria into the back seat.

"Clever how you just happened to be at Mass," Carmela said after they were settled in the car. "Somehow I don't think it was just a chance meeting."

"Tell yuh the truth, yesterday at work I *did* overhear your father tell one of his customers that you were all goin' to nine o'clock Mass, so I went to Raul's house after work and asked 'im if he wanted to go. Didn't know Gloria was go'n'a be there, too. That was just chance. And what a great coincidence. Wasn't it her idea to meet here?"

"We hadt so much fun last Sunday. I wantedt to do it again," Gloria said.

The car hop came back to take lunch orders for everybody.

"So, what is it with you?" Carmela asked. "First, you just happen to get a job in my father's barber shop? Then you start going to the same Mass we go to? Are you Catholic?"

"'Course I'm Catholic, but I don't go to Mass regular. Only went today 'cause I was hopin' to see *you*."

"Oh, really? Are you watching me?"

"Matter of fact, yeah. Wan'a get to know yuh better. Main reason I got the job, but not the only reason."

"What other reasons?"

"Shop is way too cool for him to be so slow. I think I can help him get it goin' again, like how he says it was after the war."

"Hey, Jack's a real good barber," Raul chimed in from the back seat. "Knows how to bring 'em in."

"Confident about it, isn't he?" said Gloria.

"Call it what you want," said Jack, "but I'm go'n'a be cuttin' a lota' hair, and so's Carlos. In the Navy, the guys'd rather get haircuts from me than the professionals in town when we were in port. Same thing in barber college. The other students all wanted me to cut their hair,

84

The Journeyman and the Apprentice

and I even built up a regular clientele in school. Check out Raul's taper. Ain't go'n'a find one smoother anywhere. Second haircut I did in Carlos' shop."

Raul sat forward on the seat and turned his head so the others could see his taper.

"Looks pretty goodt," Gloria admitted.

"Where you ladies wan'a go today?" Raul asked. He sat back in the seat and rested his hands on his knees.

"Nice day," Gloria said. "How about the Planetarium in Griffith Park? Beautiful view from up there!"

"'Sounds real good," Jack said. "Bet yuh can see all the way to Catalina today. Let's go."

When the car hop took the trays away and they'd paid the check, Jack backed the car out and swung it onto Fletcher Drive. He headed past Riverside Drive through Toonerville to Los Feliz. The fountain at the corner of Riverside and Los Feliz was dancing up and down.

"We ought'a come here sometime after dark when the lights are on and it changes colors," Jack said.

They drove down Los Feliz to Catalina, took a right and wound around up the mountain to a spot where they could see the city spread out below them. The downtown skyline, with

City Hall as its centerpiece, loomed on the horizon off to the left.

Then they drove back down the hill to Los Feliz and took it to Vermont where they went back up the mountain to the Planetarium. It was open to the public and there were quite a few people milling around. Inside, they walked around and looked at the various displays of the moon's surface, Saturn's rings, the schematic of the solar system. They went outside and looked at the view of the city from the outside rim of the Planetarium.

As the sun descended in the western sky, they started back to the car. When they got to Los Feliz, the sky was darkening. Dinner time was approaching, and Jack was thinking about food again.

"Hey, how 'bout we go to Bob's over in Glendale, get some Big Boys and malts," Jack said. "They got real thick malts."

"I should let my parents know," said Carmela, "but I don't know how. We don't have a telephone in the house. Only the pay phone in the barber shop."

"I needt to call my parents, too," Gloria said, "so let's call *them*, and they couldt send my little sister down to your house to tal' them what we're doeen."

The Journeyman and the Apprentice

"I'm not sure it's going to be okay with Mamá," Carmela said, scrunching into the corner where seat and door come together.

"Come on, Carmela," Gloria said leaning forward in the back seat. "Look, there's a pay phone right there. Pull over, Jack."

Jack pulled up alongside the curb. Raul got a nickel from his pocket and gave it to Gloria. Carmela went with her to the phone booth. There was rarely ever a problem with either Gloria's parents or with Carlos and Teresa. All four were casual and trusted their daughters to always do what was right. The Roybals would be conscientious and make sure that Gloria's younger sister, Martha, would go to Carmela's house to tell Carlos and Teresa what the girls were doing.

"See how easy that was," Gloria said. "Now your mom and dad won't worry."

"They won't worry, but Mamá will not be happy when Martha tells her who we're with."

"You're exaggerating."

By the time they came out of the phone booth, the sky had gone completely dark. Going to Glendale after sunset was not a good idea. Glendale cops were notorious for escorting blacks and Mexicans out of town after dark.

Jerome Arthur

They had a good time at Bob's, and the food was good. When they finished eating, Jack pulled the car out onto Colorado Boulevard, and didn't go two blocks before a squad car pulled him over.

"May I see your driver's license?" the cop said to Jack, leaning down and looking past him into the car.

"Sure," Jack replied, taking out his wallet and finding his license. As he handed it to the officer, he asked, "What's up?"

"One moment, please," the cop said, walking back to his car where he made a call on his two-way radio. When he came back, he handed the license to Jack and said,

"You didn't break any traffic laws, son, but take my advice and get these people with you back over to West Glendale, or wherever you brought 'em from. They got no business in this part of town at this hour."

Jack was incredulous. He'd heard such stories about Glendale but never believed they were really true. Carmela, Gloria, and Raul sat silently, humiliated by the cop's words, and Jack was silent too, because he'd had some experience with cops and was afraid of them with their guns and night sticks. Quietly and unobtrusively, Jack kicked the ignition button next to

The Journeyman and the Apprentice

the gas pedal and crawled slowly off down the street. He'd planned to take a cruise down Brand Boulevard to see the lights of the movie theaters and car dealers, but now he was so disheartened that he simply drove to San Fernando Road and back to Cypress Avenue in silence. He parked in front of the barber shop.

"I didn't believe that was happening to us," he said, as they sat there catching their breath after the ordeal.

"Happens all the time," Gloria said.

"Don't it just piss you off, though?"

"Chure," said Raul, "but what yuh go'n'a do 'bout it, eh? Yuh say anything and they pull their club on yuh, ese."

"Well, I think I'd better be getting upstairs," Carmela said.

"Let me walk you up," offered Jack, hopping out to go around and hold the door for her.

"Uh, no, that wouldn't be a good idea. I'll just walk up by myself, thanks."

She moved toward the stairs, and Jack started to follow, but she held up her hand indicating that he should not come along. He went back around the car, got in and chauffeured Gloria to her house, and then Raul to his.

Jerome Arthur

*　　　*　　　*

When Teresa heard a car pull up to the curb, she went to the window and looked down to see the same jalopy that had dropped the girls off last week. She watched for a minute. The driver's door opened and someone got out. She thought she knew who it was when she spotted the white panama hat in the darkness. She was sure when he stepped onto the sidewalk under the streetlight. Her expression darkened. She went back to her chair, sat down and picked up her knitting. She wanted to appear calm. Carlos was in his chair by the radio.

"So where have you been all day?" Teresa asked sternly, as Carmela entered. She was trying to sound inquisitive only; she wasn't showing the tension she truly felt.

"Gloria and I met the two boys we saw at Mass this morning at Van de Kamp's. We went up to Griffith Park, and then we went over to Glendale for hamburgers and malts. Did Martha tell you we were going to be late?"

"Oh, indeedt she didt. Isn't he the same boy who's workeen with your father? Same one you were with last Sunday?"

The Journeyman and the Apprentice

This brought Carlos out of his radio reverie. He looked back and forth between his wife and daughter.

"Yes, Mamá, he's the same one."

"Why do I have this feeling that you two are plotting something behindt my back?"

With this inclusion of him in their dialogue, Carlos suddenly was attentive to what she was saying, but he still said nothing himself.

"I don't know what you're talking about," Carmela said. "I've only been out with him twice. Gloria wanted to go out with Raul, but she didn't want to go alone, so she asked me if I'd go with her, and I did. Jack just happened to be with Raul. He's the one with the car. That's all I know about it. He's a nice boy, and I enjoy his company, but I'm not plotting anything, especially not with Papá."

"That's right." Carlos finally spoke. "I only hired a barber, thinking maybe it would help business. Last thing in my mind was to try to pick out a boyfriend for my daughter."

"Well, all I have to say to you, Miss Carmela, is that you'd better be careful who you go on dates with. I noticed that that boy diden't go to communion this morneen, and his friend didt. I diden't raise you to be getteen involved with non-Catholic gringos, so you just remember that before you break your mother's heart."

Carmela remained calm, even though her heart was racing. She didn't know quite how to respond to this, so she didn't, but rather went to her room. It was too early to be preparing for bed, so she put a record on her turntable and listened while she picked out her outfit for work on Monday morning. She didn't have any ironed blouses, so she got the iron and ironing board from the kitchen and brought them back to her room where she ironed and listened to her records. She also pondered the events of the day, and the image of Jack hovered in her imagination. She really did like him, and the two times she'd been out with him, she'd had a good time. It took her forty-five minutes to get all her clothes ironed, and then she started getting ready for bed.

In the other room, Carlos and Teresa continued their nightly ritual. Carlos didn't try to justify himself in any way to Teresa, and she didn't chastise him. She'd said her piece to Carmela, and that was enough. At ten o'clock Carlos turned the radio off, Teresa put her knitting things away, and they moved off to their room.

Six

Monday was the first cold day of the season, and the rain that night made it seem colder than it actually was. By Tuesday morning there was a steady downpour, and for all the business they did, Carlos thought he might as well not have opened the shop at all. It was so cold and dark outside that the heat and lights were on all day. The two barbers barely made enough between them to pay for the electricity they used.

"This is a real lesson in the barber business," Carlos told Jack after lunch as they sat staring out the window at the dismal day. "Typical to be slow on the first day of a rain. Customers figure a haircut can wait till it stops. End of the month, too. People get their paychecks first of the month. I'm goin' across the street and hang around with Enrique. Keep an eye on things here. Okay?"

Carlos and Contreras chatted as they watched the rain and waited for the Eight Star. The paper arrived on schedule at three-thirty, and ten minutes later, Carlos looked up from the sports section and saw a customer approach the barber shop wearing a raincoat and hat and tilting into the storm.

"Mira," Contreras said. "Eddie Herrera. Ain't yuh goeen over there, eh?"

"Naw, let the kid take 'im. That's one I can do without. Always bitching and complaining."

Carlos and Enrique watched Eddie come face to face with Jack. Barber and client were framed by the front window. Jack offered Eddie a seat in his chair.

"I'm go'n'a stick around here, read the paper, eh. By then Jack'll be done with Eddie."

"Up to you, eh. I like haveen the company. Ain't no customers keepeen me company. Not today."

A couple of rain-soaked kids came in and bought a dime's worth of candy. Carlos was almost done with the paper, but Jack still wasn't finished with Eddie's haircut. He couldn't tell if it was because Jack was laying his rap on Eddie, or because Eddie was complaining. He suspected the latter, but whatever it was, Eddie wasn't

The Journeyman and the Apprentice

getting out of the chair, so Carlos stayed with Contreras and looked for a story he hadn't read in one of the newspaper sections he'd already seen.

Eddie left the shop at four-twenty and walked across the street to the store, sending Carlos scampering into Enrique's back room. He could hear Eddie asking for a pack of Chesterfields, and he came back out front after he heard the bell on Enrique's front door jingle marking Eddie's departure. Then Carlos went back to the shop.

"Everything okay with that haircut?"

"Yuh mean Eddie? Not bad. He always bitch and piss and moan like that?"

"Yeah. That's why I didn't come back. He's too much trouble. I'm tired a' messing with 'im. Looked like you handled him real good, though."

"Oh yeah, I can handle him all right, but someday, and it's go'n'a be soon, I ain't go'n'a have time for all that bitchin'."

"You sure are confident. I hope some of it rubs off on me."

And indeed, it was rubbing off on him. For the first time in a long while, Carlos felt a developing self-assurance. Not even the slow rainy day could dampen his spirits after such a recognition. It had been a long time since he'd felt this way, and now when he tried to imagine the future, he saw a new day in which his shop would be as busy as it had been when he first moved to Cypress Park.

The two men sat around until five o'clock, and Carlos told Jack to take off if he wanted to. The only reason Jack wanted to hang around was to get a glimpse of Carmela at a quarter to six, but he knew it was her night at school, and he wouldn't be seeing her that day, so he decided to go ahead and go home.

The rain continued through Wednesday, and business was just as slow as it had been on Tuesday. By four-thirty, Carlos told Jack to take off early again.

"I'm goin' down to the bar on San Fernando. Get a quick beer," said Jack. By now the rain had lightened up. "Be back in a bit."

That would give him plenty of time to have a beer and get back to meet Carmela when she got off the streetcar.

"Okay by me," Carlos said. "Tonight I'm keeping the doors open till six."

The bar was crowded; there were no vacant barstools. After he got his beer, Jack stood near the back wall next to a guy whose name

The Journeyman and the Apprentice

was also Jack. He was a switchman in the train yard across the street.

"What do *you* do?" Jack the switchman asked Jack the barber.

"I'm a barber. Work for Carlos up on Cypress Avenue."

He set his beer down, reached for his wallet, took out a card and gave it to the switchman.

"You weren't kiddin'. Name's same as mine, ain't it? Go'n'a be needin' a haircut pretty quick. Maybe give yuh a try."

Not having a place to sit was motivation for Jack to drink up and get out of there. When he got back to Cypress, it was still fifteen minutes before Carmela's streetcar would be due, so he went into Enrique's store and picked up a couple of beers and waited there. He stepped out the door as the streetcar glided to a stop.

"Hey, how yuh doin'?" he said, as she descended to the safety zone. "Can I walk yuh home?"

"What if I said no?" she replied coyly.

"I'd do it anyway." His response was also coy.

...two can play this game....

97

She didn't say anymore as they headed toward the shop in the drizzle. When they got to the front door, she poked her head in and greeted her father who was sitting on his stool at the back of the shop with his tenor sax poised in front of him.

"We should go out sometime, maybe to a movie or something," Jack said as they got to the steps leading to the house. "Just the two of us. Wha'da yuh say?"

"I don't know," she replied. "We'd probably have to meet in secret. Mamá doesn't want me to go out with you."

"Huh? What's with that?"

"I don't know if she'll ever get over her prejudices. I'm not proud of them. Her worst one is against non-Mexicans, and she's also prejudice against non-Catholics. I'm really sorry, Jack. Papá and I will have to work on her."

"Don't be sorry. Guess I'll have to work on her, too. At least now I know what I'm up against. And the next time you talk to her about it, you can tell her that I am Catholic. My parents were staunch French-Canadian Catholics. More devout than I could ever hope to be. I was baptized when I was six months old. Used to take me to Mass every Sunday when I was little. Got into my teens and quit goin'. And yuh

98

know, come to think of it, that's about when I started getting in trouble, too. Not much I can do about the Mexican part, but if it'll help me get closer to you, I'm go'n'a start goin' to Mass again. Maybe I'll go back to confession and communion, too."

"It doesn't really matter to me, but that would definitely help with Mamá. She'll like it that you're a Catholic."

"Your dad likes me. Doesn't his opinion count for anything?"

"Not on this. She's a strong woman and Papá does not try to tell her what to do; not that he could anyway. He's just a nice, easy going guy who doesn't try to rule Mamá and doesn't let her rule him. He gets his way, but softly, and on the subject of you, he doesn't hold much sway with her. Which is strange, because he probably knows you better than any of us."

"If we ever did have a date to go to the movies or something, would we have to keep it secret from him, too?"

"I don't think so; he wouldn't mind. I don't even think we literally have to keep it a secret from Mamá. I just think it will take her some time to get used to the idea."

"We migh's well go to the movies then. Yuh wan'a, don't yuh?"

"Yes. I've had fun both times we've been together."

"How 'bout a movie this Saturday night, then?"

"Anything in particular you want to see?"

"I don't know. You go to more movies than me. Wha'da *you* wan'a see? Check the newspaper. Pick something out, and you can tell me what it is tomorrow night when you get off the streetcar. Okay?"

"All right. I'll look for you tomorrow."

She went up the steps, and Jack went back into the shop. He took the beers out of the bag and opened them. Eddie had been the last customer, so their workstations were clean. Jack headed toward the back of the shop. Just as he was about to put his jacket on, a man and his son opened the front door and came in.

"You still open?" he said to Carlos who was taking the money out of the cash register.

"Sure, come on in."

"Can you do two of us?"

"I think so. You wan'a do one more?" This to Jack.

"Sure," Jack said taking off his hat and jacket and putting his smock back on.

The Journeyman and the Apprentice

They finished the haircuts by twenty after six and drank their beers by six-thirty. They both cleaned up their workstations as they drank. Carlos wanted to be at the dinner table with Teresa, so he told Jack to go ahead and take off, and he'd sweep the floor when Teresa went back to work.

*   *   *

Thursday evening at a quarter to six Jack was standing on the sidewalk in front of the shop waiting for Carmela's streetcar to come over the rise a quarter mile down the street. The rain had stopped and the clouds had cleared. After two dismal days in a row, Jack welcomed the nice weather on the third day. It had been busy, and this turned out to be the only break he'd gotten all day. A single light appeared over the rise, and as it got closer, he could make out the straight, standing figure of the motorman. The streetcar squealed to a stop and Carmela got off, followed by three other people.

"So, what're we go'n'a see?" he asked.

"*A Streetcar Named Desire.* It's playing at the Palace on Broadway. Marlon Brando's second movie. I've already seen it, but I don't mind seeing it again. He's such a good actor. I just love him. It's a Tennessee Williams play, and he also wrote the script for the film."

"Wow, you sure know a lot about it! So, we got a date? 'Time should I pick you up?"

"The movie starts at eight o'clock, so you decide what time you want to come to the house."

"How's seven sound?"

Carmela had piqued Jack's curiosity with her knowledge. All he knew about Brando was the movie he'd gone to a couple years ago, *Viva Zapata!* which he'd seen with David and a couple of other buddies at a theater in Manila when he was in the Navy. None of those guys talked about that movie the way Carmela was talking about this one.

The first date was arranged. He'd pick her up at seven; the movie started at eight. They had plenty of time to get downtown and find a parking place. Jack would have to hustle when he got off work at five o'clock (shop hours were nine to six weekdays, eight to five Saturdays, so he'd have to count on there not being any late cuts) to get home, take a shower, and get back to Carmela's house by seven. He wanted to get there fifteen minutes early so he'd have a chance to talk to Teresa. He even made up his

The Journeyman and the Apprentice

mind to pick up a couple dozen roses, a dozen for Carmela and a dozen for her mother.

The rain had stopped by Thursday, and the sun was out, but it was cold. Indian summer had ended. Jack's handing out business cards was starting to pay off, and Friday and Saturday were just as busy as Thursday had been. Two of the haircuts he did on Saturday were referrals from two new ones he'd done on Friday.

Carlos did a few new cuts, too, and was so heartened by the sudden spurt in business at the end of the week that he started thinking seriously, perhaps more seriously than ever before, about remodeling the shop. One of his new clients on Thursday morning was an upholsterer named Harry who had a shop on Figueroa. Carlos asked him how much it'd cost to re-upholster the waiting chairs. On Thursday afternoon, Lou, the salesman from Freeman Barber Supply, stopped in, and Carlos got a price on two new barber chairs. The ones he had were about twenty years old, and Lou said he'd give him fifty dollars in trade on the new ones, so he ordered two new chairs. He had no idea how he was going to pay for them.

"One of the new haircuts I did this morning is an upholsterer," Carlos told Jack at the end of the day.

"He the one you were lookin' at the waiting chairs with."

"Yep. He quoted me twenty-five bucks apiece to re-upholster 'em. Think I'm go'n'a go 'head on and get 'em done one at a time. You wan'a take one home with yuh tonight. Drop it off tomorrow on your way to work?"

"Where's his shop?" Jack asked.

"Figueroa near Marmion. Here's his card. Address is right there."

"Shoot, that's right near my house. That'd be no problem. 'Time's he open in the mornin'?"

"Told me nine o'clock. It's okay if you're late tomorrow."

"Cool."

*   *   *

On Saturday Jack started his last haircut at four-thirty. He swept the floor and cleaned up his backbar and was out the door by five-fifteen.

"Carmela tell yuh we're goin' to a movie tonight?" he said as Carlos was paying him.

"Yeah, I heard about it. What time you pickin' her up?"

"About seven."

"Guess I'll see yuh then."

104

The Journeyman and the Apprentice

"You will."

Jack hurried home, took a shower and got ready for his date. At six-fifteen he got into his car and drove up to a flower shop in Highland Park. He got a couple dozen red roses for the two ladies. At ten to seven he pulled up in front of the shop. He climbed the steps to the house, suddenly feeling apprehensive. Carlos answered his knock.

"Hey, Jack. Come on in."

He opened the door wide, and Jack entered. Carlos put his arm on Jack's shoulder and escorted him the rest of the way into the living room. He guided him over to Teresa who was sitting at one end of the couch working her knitting needles. She put her knitting on her lap and looked up as he approached.

"You met Carmela's mother, Teresa?"

"First day on the job. Hello," he said and presented her with one of the bunches of roses.

"Oh how nice! They're beautiful!"

She graciously accepted the flowers, smiling and nodding, but she said little as she got up and made her way to the kitchen to put them in water.

"This one's for Carmela," Jack said to Carlos, as Teresa sidled past them toward the kitchen.

Jerome Arthur

Carlos offered him a seat at the other end of the davenport, and he waited for Carmela. Teresa returned from the kitchen with the roses in a green, clear-glass vase which she set down in the middle of the dining room table.

"They're beautiful," she repeated, stepping back and admiring them.

"They smell good, too," Carlos said.

Teresa sat down at her end of the davenport and resumed her knitting. After being together all week in the shop, the two men didn't have much to talk about, so the three of them sat in silence, Teresa click-clicking her needles, Jack staring straight ahead holding a dozen roses, and Carlos fumbling with the tuner on the radio.

Carmela emerged from her room, and Jack stood up, astonished at a beauty he hadn't previously seen in her. With her pink angora sweater, full skirt and high heels, she put on an appearance that contrasted sharply with her workaday look. His first glimpse at her was more of a gape than a simple look. He was momentarily silent, and he forgot to offer her the roses. Then, suddenly aware that he was staring, he closed his mouth, came to his senses and offered the flowers to her. Since it was getting

106

late, she gave them to her mother to put in water.

"Now," Teresa said, "are you coming home right after the movie or are you going out somewhere afterwards?"

"I thought we'd get something to eat after the show," Jack replied. "We won't be too late, probably not past midnight."

Teresa thought that was reasonable. Carlos wasn't at all concerned. The young people went off down the stairs, and Teresa found another vase to put Carmela's flowers in, which she set up in her room. They settled themselves, and he listened to some big band swing while Teresa knitted and listened, too.

"Well, what do you think of Jack now, mi cariña?" Carlos asked.

"I have to adtmit the flowers took me by su'prise, but I'm still not convinced that he's goeen to be any goodt to you and your business. And I still don't think it's a goodt idea for Carmela to get mixed up with a gringo."

"Gringo's a put-down. I don't see it that way. 'Fact, he's been hanging around Mexicanos so long, he talks just like one. I feel like he's just another Mexicano. And besides, who cares about all that anyway?"

"I don't trust white people ever since those gringo soldiers and sailors stripped and beat up those poor guys weareen zoot suits, and they raped their girlfriends. Mexican girls were afraidt to go downtown after that. You were off in the Navy fighteen for that."

"Come on, baby. That's ancient history. And I know about it. I read about it in the papers. I know we should never forget, but, yuh know, it's over, in the past. Leave it there."

They said no more. Carlos thought contentedly that his daughter was in good hands with Jack, whereas Teresa still felt apprehensive about Jack. Meanwhile, Jack and Carmela had a good time at the movie. They held hands and shared a box of popcorn. After the show they went to Tommy's for chili burgers and sodas, and as Jack had promised, he had Carmela home by midnight.

Seven

Jack was walking on cloud nine after his date with Carmela. He stayed awake late that night and went over it in his mind. They'd had a good talk in the car as they ate their chili burgers.

"I want to quit my job and get enrolled full-time at City College like Gloria," she said.

"Hey, it's go'n'a happen."

"How can you be so sure? We've all been working so hard since I graduated from Sacred Heart, and we can't seem to manage it."

"I'm sure 'cause I only been workin' in the shop two weeks, and business is already gettin' better. Bet you'll be full-time by spring."

"You really think so?"

"Not a doubt in my mind. Me and your dad're good barbers. Alls we got'a do is get 'em in the door, and I c'n already see that happenin'."

"Ever think about going back to school yourself?"

"Not really. Never was any good in school. I didn't even finish high school. Quit to join the Navy."

"How come?"

"Well, haven't wanted to tell yuh this part of it. Now I guess I'll hav'ta. Went in the Navy 'cause the judge made me. Gave me two choices. Either go in the military or go to juvy. I joined the Navy. 'Sides watchin' my dad when I was little is most a' what I know about cuttin' hair, and I learned more of it in the Navy. It's the only branch a' the military where you can be a barber."

"What did you do that you almost landed up in juvenile hall?"

"Hotwired a couple cars and took 'em for a drive. Second time I got caught, judge says go in the military or go to juvy."

"You should go back...get your diploma."

"I got my G.E.D. in the Navy. I could go to J.C. right now if I wanted."

"You should. You're a lot smarter than you think."

The Journeyman and the Apprentice

"If I ever did go back, Uncle Sam'd pick up the tab. G.I. bill. What I used to go through barber college."

"You really should give it some serious thought. You'd do well in college."

"How'd yuh like me to come down to City on Tuesday night? Pick yuh up and give yuh a ride home. What time's your break?"

"Eight-thirty."

"I could come then and go back to your class with yuh. Sit in, if the teacher'd let me. See how much I like it."

"You would."

"Yuh know, just 'cause I don't go to school, don't mean I don't read. Started that in the Navy. It used to get boring when we were out at sea, so I'd go down to the ship's library and check out books. I'll get interested in an author and try to read everything he wrote. Right now I'm on a John Steinbeck kick. Readin' *Cannery Row*. Funny book."

"Wouldn't your parents like to see you get a college education?" she asked.

"Shoot, I ain't got no parents, unless you count David's. Mine died in a car wreck right after I went to boot camp. Not too long after that, I met the Pachecos."

Jerome Arthur

"Gee, I'm awfully sorry about your parents."

"Thanks. Good people. Maybe a little too good for me. They sure put up with a lot when I was a teenager. Always managed to talk my way outa' most of the trouble I got into. There's a lot they didn't know about."

"You really do like to talk. You have such an outgoing personality. It was obvious to me when we met, the way you walked right up to us that first day, and the way you talked Papá into giving you a job when he didn't even have enough work for himself."

"I think I picked that up from my dad. He was a real sweet talkin' son of a gun. Great barber with a gift a' gab."

"Who are the Pachecos?"

"Me and David were bunk mates in boot camp, and then we both got into ship's service on board the Kearsarge. His family sorta' took me in when I went home with him on leave. Good people. That's where me and Raul went last Sunday before we met you and Gloria at the drive-in."

"Is that where you learned Spanish?"

"Some. They speak mostly Spanish in that house."

112

The Journeyman and the Apprentice

They finished eating, and it was already eleven-thirty. Jack remembered what he'd told Teresa about being home before midnight, so he started the car up and began the trip back across town.

"I'm going to start giving you books to read," Carmela said as they drove through Chinatown on North Broadway.

What he liked most about that idea was that it would establish a connection between them. If she was going to give him books to read, he'd at least be seeing her when she did it.

"That'd be real swell. Me 'n' Raul'll see you guys tomorrow at Mass."

"That'll make Gloria happy."

"Not you?"

"Yes, me too," she said, rolling her eyes in faux exasperation.

When he stopped the car at the curb in front of the barber shop, he leaned over and kissed her, and then he hastily got out and held the door for her. Because she hadn't resisted the first time, he kissed her longer at her front door. When the door closed behind her, he bounded down the steps, taking them two at a time.

Back at his place he lay in bed thinking about the evening, basking in the afterglow of his thoughts. Carmela, meanwhile, experienced a tingling sensation when she walked into her room in the dark, and caught the scent of the roses in the vase on her dresser. Her heart leaped when she turned the light on and saw them.

*   *   *

The next morning Jack drove to Raul's house, picked him up, and they went to nine o'clock Mass. On the ride to church, Jack told Raul about his date. He got so excited in the telling that he was stumbling over his own words. The Rángels were all there again with Señora Guevara and Gloria, but this time Teresa reacted differently toward the boys. Of course Jack had a different attitude, too. Before saying anything to Carlos, he greeted Teresa.

"Buenos días, Señora Rángel," he said, drawing a look of surprise from Señora Guevara. He spoke the language like a Mexican.

"Good morning, Jack," Teresa said. "Thank you for bringeen my baby home before midnight as you hadt promised."

Her delivery was flat, more matter of fact than emotional. Then she moved on into the church with her mother. Jack then spoke to Carlos as Raul and Gloria started their own con-

114

The Journeyman and the Apprentice

versation. Carmela was standing next to her father as he spoke with Jack about the waiting chair at the upholsterer's. Then they all followed Teresa and her mother into the church. They took the same positions in the pews as they had the previous Sunday, only this time Raul and Gloria joined Carlos and Jack, keeping their seats during the celebration of the Eucharist, thus leaving the three generations of women to be the only recipients from their group.

As they stood out in front of the church after Mass, Gloria announced that she and Raul were going to walk to her house, and she suggested that Jack pick him up there in a little while. This prompted Jack to offer the Rángels a ride home. Teresa showed some reticence, but Carlos convinced her to accept the offer, so the three older people got into the back seat, Carlos and Teresa flanking her mother. Carmela rode up front with Jack.

"Where should I take Señora Guevara?" he asked.

"Just take her with us," Carlos said.

"Wan'a go for a little Sunday drive before I drop you guys off, or yuh j'st wan'a go straight home?"

"I ain't never been on a Sunday drive in a car, eh."

115

"Tell yuh what. We'll just cruise up Figueroa to where the upholsterer is and then back to your place. It's only a fifteen-minute drive. You can check out the shop your chair is gettin' fixed in."

"Sounds good," Carlos said, looking at Teresa. "Let's go."

She shrugged, and away they went.

"¿Donde vamos?" Señora Guevara asked as they headed east on Cypress.

"Un paseo en coche," Teresa replied.

As Jack had said, it wasn't a long drive, and he had them back to their house a half hour after they'd left the church. Teresa thought the car would break down any minute, but it didn't. It only looked like a jalopy; it ran good. The car was a deluxe model and quite luxurious when it was new. The radio in the dashboard still worked perfectly, the knobs and push buttons all fully functional. The engine was in great shape. It didn't burn any oil. Jack changed it himself every three-thousand miles and did tune-ups every ten-thousand miles. The car was just old and the body hadn't been kept up. Dented fenders had gone unrepaired. It was mechanically sound; it just *looked* like a heap, and the unsuspecting first time passenger, like Teresa, was reluctant to get in. It's breaking down never

116

even entered Jack's mind. As far as he could tell, they all enjoyed the ride.

At the shop he hopped out and ran around to the other side like a chauffeur and opened both doors. Then the biggest surprise of the morning. Teresa invited him up to have breakfast with the family. Forgetting completely about Raul, he accepted the invitation and, with Carmela at his side, climbed the stairs behind the other three. In the house Jack joined Carlos in the front room while Carmela played the piano for them, and Teresa and her mother went into the kitchen to make the coffee and heat some pan dulce in the oven. They also fixed some chorizo con huevos.

"You know, Carlos, I been thinking. Maybe we oughta' put up a sign outside the shop advertising flat tops, like John. Wha'da yuh think?"

"Now that you're in the shop and can do flat tops, that's not a bad idea. Prob'ly bring in some new customers, and maybe bring back some I lost because I ain't been doin' flat tops."

"Hey, no reason you can't do 'em. They're easy as hell. Oops!" He put his hand over his mouth as a way of apologizing for his language.

Carlos waved his hand nonchalantly. "Ah, don't worry about it, guy. I talk like that, too. It's not the first time Carmela's heard that kind of language."

Teresa and Señora Guevara emerged from the kitchen, one carrying a tray with a steaming pot and some cups, the other carrying a tray with two plates, one with hot pan dulce covered with a clean hand towel to keep them warm, the other with the chorizo con huevos. They put them down on the dining room table. Carlos, Carmela and Jack stood up and moved to the dining room. Just as they were sitting down, the doorbell rang, and Teresa answered it. Standing at the front door were Raul and Gloria. She invited them in, and Raul said,

"I thought you forgot about me, so we came up here."

"I guess I did," said Jack.

"Vamos a desayunarnos," Teresa said. "Wouldt you like to join us?"

The dining room table was a large round oak affair with the center leaf permanently installed and had six chairs around it. Teresa got an extra chair out of Carmela's room and the two young people joined them. They all chatted and drank coffee. Spanish and English intermingled so that Jack and Señora Guevara at the two

The Journeyman and the Apprentice
extremes were both able to participate. Occasionally Jack communicated directly to her in his broken Spanish which delighted and impressed her.

"What made you decide you wanted to be a barber?" Teresa asked Jack at one point.

"Did Carmela tell you my dad was a barber? Worked in a shop in Yosemite Village up in Eagle Rock. When I was a little kid, I passed his shop on my way home from school. I'd stop and hang around, watch him cut hair. My buddies'd come with me. Guy he worked for had Tootsie-pop suckers, and he'd always give us some. It was a fun place to hang around. While my buddies read comics, I'd watch Pop. He was a real pro."

"Carmela says you're parents were from French Canada."

"That's right. Came from Quebec. Moved here right after they got married."

"So sorry you lost them. Carmela told me about it."

"Thanks for your sympathy. I miss 'em. They didn't speak no English when they first got here, but they learned it quick. He was already a licensed barber up in Canada, but California ain't got reciprocity. He had to take a refresher course at Moler Barber College down

119

Main Street. That all happened before I was born. Told me that story a lota' times. Said they called him 'the Parisian' in barber college."

"What was your father's name?"

"Etienne Niel. Mom's name was Monique."

"So why is it you don't have a French name like your parents."

"I do. Jean-Luc. Folks've always just called me Jack. I was born at the French Hospital down Chinatown."

Everybody else at the table was listening to Jack and Teresa, even Señora Guevara, which led him to believe that she understood more English than she let on. Shortly after he finished telling it, she announced that she was going to go home, and Jack offered her a ride.

"Maybe you ladies'd like to go for a ride with me and Raul after we drop your grandma off. Wha'da yuh say?"

Carmela looked to her mother for approval, and Teresa made no objection, so the four young people and the old woman went down to the car and drove off. Carlos helped Teresa clear the dining room table, and when they sat down in the living room, he said,

"Jack's not such a bad guy for a gavacho, huh?"

120

The Journeyman and the Apprentice

"I might have been too quick in my first judgment of him."

She picked up her knitting and he turned on the radio. He only listened for a few minutes before turning it off and getting up and going out for a walk. He walked down the street, and when he got to John's shop, he found John inside cleaning up.

"How's it going, John?"

"Pretty good, Carlos. How's about yourself?"

"Not bad. Did yuh know, I brought in an apprentice a couple weeks ago?"

"Yeah. I saw you guys the other day on my way home for lunch. Workin' out okay?"

"So far, so good. Seems like business is already getting better. He's real good with flat tops."

"Yeah. It's the style. Yuh got'a be able to do 'em. A lot of our business is flat tops."

"I'm getting better at doing 'em since Jack's been there."

"Jack, huh? Gavacho?"

"Uh huh, but he speaks real good Spanish, and he's got one hell of a personality. Bringing in a lota' new customers."

"Órale! That's good, eh."

"How're you guys doin'?"

121

"Shoot, we're busy all the time. Sometimes I got'a pull myself away just to get some lunch. They stack up on us."

"That's good."

Carlos and John talked for another five minutes, and then Carlos headed back on the other side of the street. He passed the house, the Foix bread company and the Ralston Purina plant, continuing all the way up to the gas station at Verdugo Road before crossing the street again and heading home. When he went inside, he found Teresa on the couch working her knitting needles.

"Where didt you go?" she asked.

"Oh, just for a walk. John was doing some Sunday cleaning so I stopped and talked to him. I back tracked up to Verdugo and then back here. Lazy Sunday out there. Not much goin' on. How long're the kids go'n'a be gone?"

"Don't know. If it's anything like the last time, it won't be till after dark."

She continued her knitting, and he picked up Friday's *La Opinión,* which Carmela had brought home, and he read a couple stories.

Right around sunset Jack's car pulled up to the curb down below, and as they heard their footsteps climbing the stairs, Teresa got up to go to the front door, but Carlos motioned her to sit

122

The Journeyman and the Apprentice

down. They heard the door open and Carmela came in. Jack's footsteps retreated down the stairs, and the car pulled away from the curb.

"Where didt you go?" Teresa asked.

"No place special. We just drove around. Gloria and I took them over to City College, and we walked around campus. Showed Jack where my class is. He's picking me up on Tuesday night. He's coming at the break, so he can observe the last half of my class. I'd like to see him get interested in college. He's a really smart boy, and I think he would do well, but right now he's not interested."

"Well, I'm certainly more impressed with him since I talked to him. I think you two might've been right about him and I was wrong."

And with that Carmela went off to her room to listen to records. Carlos and Teresa wiled away the evening in the living room.

*   *   *

On Tuesday Jack tried to keep his anticipation at meeting Carmela in check. He went to the bar at the end of the day and had a quick beer before going home for something to eat. At a quarter to eight, he got in the car and headed over to City. The class was going out on break as he approached. Carmela and another girl were walking toward him.

"Hi, Jack," she said when they met.

"How's it goin'?"

"This is Delia," she said, introducing her friend.

"Hi, Delia."

"Hi."

They walked to the cafeteria, and Jack treated them to Cokes.

Back in class Carmela went to the teacher to get permission for Jack to sit in. He only got to hear the teacher lecture for fifteen minutes. The class had a writing assignment from nine to ten. During that time, Jack wandered around campus. Then he went out onto Vermont Avenue and headed up to the corner at Santa Monica Boulevard and looked in the window of the barber shop there. It looked like it had been recently remodeled, new floor, fresh paint, new chairs. He checked it out for ideas he could tell Carlos about. He got back to campus at a quarter to ten just as Carmela was handing in her essay.

"Were you the first one finished?" he asked as they headed away from campus.

"Mm hm."

124

The Journeyman and the Apprentice

"Wow. That's pretty good. What kinda' grade you gettin'?"

"Probably an 'A.'"

"Wha'da yuh mean 'probably'?"

"Well, that's the only grade I've gotten on anything I've turned in, so I think it will take a major catastrophe for me to get anything less. What did you think of the teacher's lecture?"

"Okay, but I only heard him for fifteen minutes. Don't know if I could sit still for a whole semester. I know I'd never be as good a student as you."

"You'd get interested once you started. You'd be surprised how infectious it can be."

"We'll see."

They pulled up in front of the shop at ten-fifteen, and he walked with her to the top of the stairs. He kissed her goodnight and drove home.

Eight

Mid morning the Tuesday before Thanksgiving Teresa went to her mother's house, and the two ladies made plans for the holiday.

"¿Are you going to invite that joven simpático, Jack, to Thanksgiving?" Señora Guevara asked. "Me gusta mucho."

"That's a good idea, Mamá. Me gusta, también. I worried about him at first. I didn't know what sus intenciones were acerca de Carmela, but now that he has told me about él mismo, I feel más mejor about him."

"¿Why didn't you like him in the beginning?" Señora Guevara asked her daughter.

"Oh, Mamá, no se. I didn't trust him mostly porque es un gringo, y también porque I didn't think he was un católico, pero Carmela has told me that he es católico."

The Journeyman and the Apprentice

"Es un muchacho tan simpático, and he speaks Spanish muy bueno. If he is not un mexicano, he surely talks como un mexicano."

"Yes he does. Bueno. I'll tell Carlitos to invite him. ¿What time will you come in the morning to help me with the food?"

"I will come a las nueve, mijita."

By the time Teresa left to go home, she was tense from the concentration of speaking Spanish. The walk back to her house relaxed the tension. As she approached the barber shop, she noticed that Carlos didn't have a customer in his chair, so she stuck her head in the door and called him outside. Jack was doing a haircut.

"I was just down at Mamá's, and we were planneen Thanksgiving dinner. She wants us to invite Jack. So, can you do that?"

"Actually, I was thinking the same thing. I'll talk to 'im."

"Goodt. Let me know if he can come."

She went up to the house, and Carlos went back into the barber shop. After Jack finished the haircut, and as he was putting his tools away, Carlos approached him.

"What're yuh doin' on Thursday?"

"Only plans I got are goin' over David Pacheco's house, but there's no set time. What's up?"

"Teresa asked me to invite you over here. She and her mother got big plans. You wan'a come over?"

"Sure. I'll go over David's after. Maybe even take Carmela so she could meet him and his family. I know they wan'a meet her."

"So, you wan'a come?"

"Sure. What time?"

"Teresa wants us at the table by three. How 'bout noon?"

"'Sounds good."

A customer came in and sat in Carlos' chair. Jack started to sweep the floor. When he finished, he got ready to leave.

"I'm goin' over Pax on Broadway. Get a pastrami. Want me to pick up something for you?"

"Nothing to eat, but since you're go'n'a be out and about, think yuh could pick up that last waiting chair over the upholstery shop? Called Harry yesterday. Said he was done with it."

Over the last three weeks, Jack had taken the waiting chairs, one at a time, to Harry's shop to get re-upholstered. Two were done; now the last one was done and needed to be picked up.

"No problem. I'll do that before I go to Pax."

128

The Journeyman and the Apprentice

"Here's twenty-five bucks. Make sure yuh get a receipt for my taxes."

"Okay."

After he picked up the chair, he drove to Lincoln Heights and got his pastrami. As he ate, he thought he'd rather be having lunch with Carmela, and he decided right then that he'd do that on Wednesday. He finished his pastrami and headed back to the shop.

When he got there, Carlos was working on a haircut, and another guy was waiting. He set the waiting chair down and stepped back to look at all three of them lined up. They looked sharp.

"Guy does nice work, huh?" Carlos said. "Looks like he cleaned and polished the chrome again, and that brown naugahyde looks like real leather."

"Yeah, came out good," Jack said as he wrapped his customer up in the haircloth.

Carlos finished the haircut he was doing, swept the floor and left the shop to go upstairs and have some lunch. After he'd eaten, he went back to the shop and found Jack working on another haircut, a flat top. He'd just started, so Carlos watched him do it, taking particular note when he rounded the upper corners using his electric clippers free hand. Carlos didn't need

129

instruction in how to do a good, clean arch over the ears with the razor, so when Jack lathered the guy around the ears, he went across the street and hung around with Contreras.

"Man, that vato wasn't kiddeen when he said he was go'n'a get busy, huh?" Enrique said as Carlos entered the market. "I been watcheen, and there's been a lot more guys goeen into your shop since he started workeen there, eh."

"Yeah, no doubt about it. He's helping me turn it around."

"What about Teresa? She likeen him better, eh?"

"You tell me. She invited him to our place for Thanksgiving."

Señora Guevara came into the store just then, not paying any attention to the two men, walking back to the canned goods section and picking up a can of Ortega chiles. As she set her purchase on the counter, she noticed for the first time that her son-in-law was there.

"¿You remember Jack, el joven quien trabaja conmigo?" he said.

"Sí."

"He's coming a nuestra casa for Thanksgiving dinner. I just invited him this morning."

"Bueno. That will be muy simpático."

The Journeyman and the Apprentice

She paid Enrique for her chiles and left the market. Carlos followed her out. When he got back to the shop, Jack had another new customer. He thought how nice it was to be making money without having to do the work himself.

Since that first time when Jack picked up Carmela at school, he'd made the practice his Tuesday night ritual. That night he was especially excited about it because he wanted to be the one to tell her that her mother had invited him to the house for Thanksgiving dinner.

"You sure it was Mamá?"

She could hardly believe her mother had come that far.

"Positive. Your dad tol' me she was the one."

They talked the whole way home, both expressing their astonishment at how much progress Teresa was making in her attitude toward Jack. For his part Jack didn't mention his plan to take Carmela out to lunch on Wednesday. He thought he'd surprise her

*   *   *

The next day started out deathly slow, unusual for a day before a holiday. The morning slipped by without a single customer coming

131

through the door. At eleven-thirty Jack told Carlos he was taking an early lunch, but he didn't tell him why. By twenty to twelve he was going south on North Broadway heading into downtown. He found a parking space two blocks from where Carmela worked.

He approached the entrance of her building at twelve noon. She was coming out with a dark-complexioned young man who was very animated, waving his arms as he talked to her. She looked like she was having a good time. Before she caught a glimpse of him, he stepped back behind one of the columns in the façade of the building. He was jealous watching her walk with the guy and looking like she was having such a good time. When he stepped back out, all he saw were their backs moving off down the street, the guy's arms still waving as he talked. Jack saw Carmela's radiant smile flash on her profile when she looked at the young man next to her.

Since Jack was already downtown, he decided to go have an Orange Julius at the stand at Seventh and Broadway behind the State Theater. He'd parked the car not far from there. The Orange Julius was good, but it didn't lift his spirits any. It wasn't like he and Carmela were going steady or anything like that, so he realized

The Journeyman and the Apprentice

that his feelings were unreasonable, but that didn't make him feel any the less jilted. How was he to know there was nothing between Carmela and the young man?

...what'm i worried about; it's only a lunch date...guy probably works in her office....

When Jack got back to the shop, Carlos was doing a haircut. It was his first of the day.

...boy, what a day...slower'n molasses in january and then I see carmela goin' to lunch with some other vato....

He didn't say anything to Carlos; he sat down in the newly upholstered waiting chair and stuck his face in a magazine, but he wasn't reading. All he could think of was Carmela with the other guy. Business never did pick up that day, and by three o'clock Jack just had to get out of there. He straightened up his backbar and told Carlos he was leaving. For the first time since their movie date a month ago, he wouldn't be in the shop or on the sidewalk when Carmela got off the streetcar and passed the front door. Carlos didn't object but did notice Jack's hangdog expression. Jack looked back at the shop as he crossed the street. The electric barber pole turning happily in its glass cylinder seemed antithetical to his mood. He felt like it was mocking him.

Jerome Arthur

At ten to six when Carmela passed her father's front window, she looked inside, and not seeing Jack, asked Carlos where he was. At first she was surprised to not find him waiting for her outside. That had been his routine on slow days for the past couple of weeks, so she didn't think much of it when Carlos told her that Jack had gone home early.

"I hope he's not sick," she said. "Is he still coming tomorrow."

"Oh, yeah. It was just slow, so he left."

She went upstairs while her father secured the shop. He followed, feeling less encouraged than he had yesterday when they'd both been so busy. This was the day before a holiday. It was supposed to be busy.

Jack, meanwhile, had gone to the bar down on San Fernando. He got there an hour and a half before the after-work rush, and he stayed through the afternoon and into early evening. He had ten beers and when he staggered out at six-thirty, he needed the walk back to his car to clear his head. The beer was making him feel better than the Orange Julius had earlier, although it was also intensifying his injured feelings.

At home he felt like he was drowning in the quiet and solitude of his little cottage. He

The Journeyman and the Apprentice

couldn't even stir himself to fix something to eat, even though he was famished, and he knew that food would take the edge off his high. Instead, he went to the refrigerator and opened a beer. That was the one that took him from buzz to drunk. He had one more and then he passed out on his bed with his clothes on. He woke up at one in the morning, feeling cottonmouth.

...amazing how so much liquid can make your mouth feel so dry....

He got off the bed and filled a glass with water and drank it down. His stomach was rumbling. The only real meal he'd had all day was breakfast which had been some sixteen hours earlier. The few hours sleep he'd gotten had sobered him some, so he decided to take a ride over to Seventh Street on the east side to a taco stand he knew was open all night.

...too bad it ain't sunday...could get some menudo...just have to settle for a burrito....

As he approached Cypress Avenue on Figueroa, he decided to take a swing past the shop, see if maybe the lights were still on in the house. He didn't know what he'd do if they were, but he wanted to see anyway. There was no traffic on Cypress, and as he passed the shop, he looked up at the house and saw that the lights were out. He turned around and headed for the taco stand on Seventh Street. For so late at night, there were quite a few people hanging around there. He ordered a chile verde burrito and a soda, and as he sat at one of the benches, a couple of the young punks started hassling him, so he picked up his meal and finished it in the car on the drive home.

*   *   *

After dinner that night Carmela went down to Gloria's house. She was surprised to find Raul there.

"I ran into him downtown when I got off the Whittier Boulevard streetcar," Gloria explained, "so we rodte the Five Eagle Rock home together, and I invitedt him to dinner."

"Jack's going down your pad tomorrow, huh?" Raul said.

"Yes he is, and later the two of us are going to visit the Pachecos."

"Oh? You met David and his family?"

"Not yet. Tomorrow will be the first time. I'm looking forward to it."

"Yeah, they're good folks. You'll like 'em."

"Who are they?" Gloria asked.

136

The Journeyman and the Apprentice

"David's a vato Jack met in the Navy," Raul said. "His family kinda' took Jack in after his parents died."

"So, are you having Thanksgiving with your family tomorrow?" Carmela asked Raul.

"Yeah, it'll be a big family gathering. My aunts and uncles'll be there and their kids. After dinner I'm coming down here to hang around with Gloria and her folks for a while, which was prob'ly more Martha's idea than anybody else's. She's the one brought it up. Gloria pushed for it, 'n' I thought, why not?"

"I think Martha likes him," Gloria said.

"She's a good kid," Raul said.

All this talk about her and Raul was making Martha blush. He stayed for another ten minutes, and then he left to catch the streetcar home. Martha walked with him up to the corner and waited until his streetcar came.

"Seems like your seeing a lot of Raul lately."

"He's a nice boy, and he's a lot of fun to be with. How are things with you and Jack?"

"I think he's mad at me."

"What happened?"

"I'm not sure. I haven't seen him since last night. It felt like he was avoiding me today. He wasn't at the shop when I got home from work. First time he's done that in a month. I hope we still have a date tomorrow. If we do, would you and Raul like to go with us? I'll mention it to Jack. I'm sure he'll be glad to have you."

"If you guys invite us, we'll go."

"I'll talk to Jack when I see him tomorrow."

They talked and listened to records. Carmela went home at a little after nine. The traffic on Cypress Avenue was light at that hour, but she could hear the cars zipping along two blocks away down on San Fernando Road. The sound of a train whistle overrode the car noise. Carlos was in his easy chair and Teresa was in her place on the couch when Carmela entered the house. He was listening to a Mexican radio station; she was knitting and listening, too.

"How is Gloria?" Teresa asked.

"Fine. Raul was there, and he's going to her house tomorrow. They're going with us to visit the Pachecos."

"What time will that be?"

"Probably when we finish eating."

"You're goeen to have a busy day."

"I'm going to bed right now."

She went to her room and stacked a couple of forty-fives on her record player. She lis-

The Journeyman and the Apprentice
tened as she got ready for bed. Shortly after she
got under the covers and started reading, Carlos
and Teresa turned off the lights and radio and
moved off to their room. By ten-fifteen the
house was dark.

*   *   *

Jack's cottage was just as lonely and deserted when he got home as it had been when
he'd left it. He took his clothes off, brushed his
teeth and got under the covers. He slept straight
through until eight in the morning, and when he
woke up, he had a grinding headache. The first
thing that came to mind was Carmela and the
young man. He banished the thought and started
getting ready to go to her house. He took a couple of aspirin with his coffee, and gradually his
headache disappeared.

*...i hope i ain't got beer breath...i
'member the navy and how that cook, ayers,
used to show up at muster smelling like a brew-
ery...wouldn't want any rangels, especially teresa, to be smelling me like that....*

"Boy, what'd you do last night?" Carlos
asked as he greeted Jack at the front door. "You
look like you were shot at and missed and shit at
and hit."

"Yeah, I guess I had a few too many beers. Can yuh smell it on me?"

"No, but yuh look rough as a cob."

"I feel rough as a cob."

As he spoke the words, Carmela came out of the kitchen where she'd been helping her mother and grandmother prepare Thanksgiving dinner.

"Happy Thanksgiving, Jack," she said.

Nine

Carmela had been wondering why Jack hadn't spoken to her since Tuesday night. She was surprised when he hadn't been waiting for her in front of the shop on Wednesday when she got off the streetcar. She was beginning to think he was avoiding her, and she didn't know why. She had no idea that Jack had spotted her going to lunch with the young man who worked with her at the insurance company.

Now it was Thanksgiving, and Jack hadn't said five words to her since he told her he'd been invited. She was aware of his stand-offishness immediately when she came into the room.

"Happy Thanksgiving," he said, giving her a cursory hug. "How yuh been?"

As they were greeting each other, Carlos went into the kitchen and joined his wife and mother-in-law. Carmela led Jack into the living room where they took seats on the couch.

"I'm fine. How are *you*?"

"Fine. Just busy is all."

He averted his gaze downward, unable to look her in the eye, embarrassed by his lie.

"Oh? Papá says it was slow yesterday."

Now it was her turn to look down, but her look was one of sadness and disappointment, not embarrassment, and Jack was beginning to feel like a heel.

"Why are you acting this way, Jack? What happened?"

"Nothin'."

"Why are you being so curt with me?"

"I don't know what yuh mean."

"I think you do."

"Maybe I like you more'n you like me."

"What's that supposed to mean?"

"You got a boyfriend?" he blurted.

"Why would you ask a question like that? I thought *you* were my boyfriend."

"I wanted to surprise yuh yesterday at work and take yuh to lunch. Know what I saw when I got to the insurance company you work at?"

"I *don't* know. What did you see?"

142

The Journeyman and the Apprentice

"You came outa' the building with a guy."

"Oh, for crying out loud. Is that what's bothering you? That was a boy named José, and he doesn't even work there anymore. Yesterday was his last day. He kept pestering me to go out to lunch, so I finally gave in and went with him. I only did it because I knew he was leaving. I probably won't ever see him again."

Jack's heart soared when he heard this, and at the same time, he felt the foolishness of his petty jealousy. He was at a loss for something to say. What he really wanted to do was to find some place to hide.

"*Was* nice to hear you say I'm your boyfriend. Didn't know yuh felt that way about me."

"It's true. Do you think I'm your girlfriend?"

"Heck yeah."

"So, are you going to introduce me to your friends, the Pachecos, today? Are we still going there?"

"I was planning on it. It's go'n'a be so cool. I already told 'em all about you."

"I'm looking forward to it."

Just then Carlos came out into the living room.

"The bird's been in the oven a couple hours now," he said. "Couple more hours and it's done."

Carmela flashed Jack the kind of smile he'd been looking for. The tension had evaporated. They sat and watched the traffic on the street below. A streetcar with only a handful of riders glided by. As it passed through the intersection, sparks flashed from its trolley.

"Wait'll yuh see the turkey enchiladas my mother-in-law makes. Enrique and María Elena Contreras'll be here pretty quick."

Señora Guevara had arrived at the house, as she'd promised, at nine o'clock. She and Teresa had the turkey in the oven by ten. Carmela had joined them by eleven and got busy making pumpkin and mince meat pies. Carlos was doing backup. If they needed something that wasn't right there, he'd get it for them, whether it was half-and-half from the Gateway on Cypress or vinegar from the pantry next to the service porch.

A half hour after the Contrerases arrived, Carmela led Jack out of the house and down the steps.

"Where we goin'?" he asked when they reached the sidewalk.

The Journeyman and the Apprentice

"I don't know. It's such a nice day. Let's walk down to the park on Pepper Street."

"Okay."

"Papá's really been a lot happier since you came to work for him," she said as they passed John's shop. "His attitude has changed. He used to be so taciturn and sullen. Now he talks constantly about his plans for the shop. I love to see him like this."

"Yeah, me too. Business has been good, which I predicted."

As they approached Gloria's street, Carmela remembered that she wanted to ask Jack if Gloria and Raul could go with them to David's house.

"That's a great idea. They like Raul. I bet they'd like to see 'im, and I know they'd like to meet Gloria."

They stopped at Gloria's house. She and her mother were busy in the kitchen, so they stayed just long enough to tell her the plan.

At the park a couple guys were shooting baskets on the blacktop court, and four more were playing touch football on the field. Jack and Carmela sat down in the grass on the side-lines. A few other couples were lounging in various places around the big lawn, and other people were passing through.

"How did you end up in the Optimist Home?" Carmela asked.

"Told yuh. For hotwiring cars. It's embarrassing. 'Fact I prob'ly shouldn't 'a' tol' yuh as much as I already did. I did some dumb stuff when I was a teenager. I was such a punk."

"That bad, huh?"

"That bad and worse."

"It must've been hard for your parents."

"Yeah. They're the ones I feel the worst about, 'specially since they died a short time after the second bust. They never got the chance to see how good I turned out."

"What a sweet thing to say."

"See why I didn't wan'a tell yuh? That's all in the past."

"How was it at the Optimist Home? Like *Oliver Twist*?"

"Who's that?"

"It's the title of a novel by Charles Dickens about a boy named Oliver Twist who's mistreated in an orphanage."

"It wasn't that bad, probably not much different'n where you went to school. Only difference was we were sorta' confined to the grounds. Kinda' like what I imagine a boarding school must be like."

"Feel like you got a good education?

146

The Journeyman and the Apprentice

"Good enough. For me, the fun part was learning how to box with the Police Athletic League. But then *that* turned into a problem for me, too."

"Oh, why?"

"I's too good at it. Won every fight. Hit another kid real hard once. Gave 'im a concussion. Hurt 'im bad. Quit after that. When they heard about it in the Navy, they wanted me to get on the ship's boxing team, but I couldn't do it. Gave me a real hard time when I didn't join. Another lifetime." Jack's voice got low and distant, and he stared off at the guys playing football. "As far as the education? I'm sure I didn't learn half as much as you, stuff like *Oliver Twist*, or words like taciturn and sullen."

"Really? You didn't understand those words when I used them?"

"Not really, but I kinda' figured it out from what you were talkin' about."

"I was talking about how uninterested and sad Papá was before you went to work in his shop. Taciturn means silent; sullen is gloomy."

"Yeah, well, I figured that out from what you were sayin'."

"You're so smart, Jack. You really ought to think about going to college."

147

"Yuh don't need a college education to cut hair."

She could tell by his response that it still wasn't the right time to bring it up, so she didn't pursue it. It was time for them to return home, so they got up and started back.

The house was redolent of the aroma of cooking turkey as they entered. María Elena Contreras was telling Señora Guevara and Teresa about a Cantínflas movie that was playing at the Million Dollar theater, and Enrique was telling Carlos how he'd gone down to Central Chevrolet to look at used cars. He said he'd seen Dick Lane on a television commercial slapping the fender of a Chevy he thought looked pretty good, so he went down to check it out. He wanted to buy it, but he didn't think he could afford it.

Leaving the adults in the living room, Carmela took Jack to her room and showed him her collection of forty-fives. He pulled out "Ain't It a Shame" and asked her to put it on. After the first two bars played, he took her by the hand and started doing the choke with her. By the end of the song, Señora Contreras and Señora Guevara were standing outside the bedroom door watching them. They both applauded and told them to do some more. Carmela put

148

The Journeyman and the Apprentice

"Why do Fools Fall in Love?" on the turntable, and she and Jack started up again. When they finished that dance, Carmela sat down on her bed, and Jack sat in the chair. They were both out of breath. The two women went back into the living room.

At two-thirty the turkey came out of the oven, and Teresa set it on the counter. Señora Guevara carved some breast and finished making her enchiladas. Carlos carved the rest and put the light and dark slices on a platter which Teresa set in the middle of the table. They all took their seats and said grace.

When Jack finished his first helping of turkey, Señora Guevara moved off to the kitchen. It was time to take the enchiladas out of the oven, so she put some on a plate and returned to the table. Jack was feeling full, but he made room for at least one enchilada. As the others finished their first helpings, they served themselves enchiladas, too. When they had all eaten their fill, they sat back and relaxed, waiting for the pies on the windowsill to cool. Teresa and her mother cleared the table and set out clean plates and forks.

Shortly before twilight, Jack and Carmela got ready to leave for David's house. After bidding everybody there a happy Thanksgiving, they drove down to Gloria's place where they picked up her and Raul. Night had fallen by the time they got to the Pachecos. They lived in a California bungalow just off Soto Street. As the four young people mounted the steps to the porch, the front door opened and David and his parents came out to greet them.

"¿Como le va, Mamá?" Jack said, hugging Señora Pacheco.

After shaking hands with David and his father, he introduced the two girls to them and to David's mother and sister, Margarita. Then Raul shook hands all around, and they went into the house. Carmela was impressed with how neat and open the place seemed. There were no trappings of the traditional American Thanksgiving. Instead, Señora Pacheco had a pot of beans cooking on the stove and she warmed up some flour tortillas and pork chile verde. The Pachecos carried on like it was just another day. Carmela liked it. Even though they were all full of turkey and other assorted Thanksgiving goodies, they had some chile verde and beans and tortillas. The four of them visited for over an hour. Carmela and Señora Pacheco talked at length about Jack. The older woman had nothing but good to say about the son she'd person-

The Journeyman and the Apprentice

ally adopted after David had brought him home on his first weekend liberty from boot camp.

Carmela listened deferentially. She wanted to tell her how much she liked him too, but she didn't. She was embarrassed to say such things to anybody but Jack himself. When they got up to leave, Señora Pacheco told Jack to bring them all back again soon. Jack drove them back across town, and when they got to Carmela's house, Señora Guevara and the Contrerases had gone home. The four young people visited with Carlos and Teresa for a while, and then Jack and Raul dropped Gloria off at her house. After he took Raul home, Jack went home himself.

Ten

The barber shop was busy the Friday after Thanksgiving, and it stayed busy all through December until Christmas. Jack had a regular clientele now, a lot of repeat business and those customers were referring new ones all the time. Carlos was noticing the return of some people he hadn't seen for a long time. He was sure a lot of them had been getting haircuts from John and Bob down the street. Some of them were coming back to Carlos, and some were going to Jack, referrals from some of his newly established clientele.

During the Christmas holidays Jack took Carmela to another movie, though it was questionable who was taking whom. It was Carmela's idea to go, and it was she who had motives other than just going out on a simple movie date. This time it was another Brando movie, *Julius Caesar*. Carmela not only wanted to see it because it was a Marlon Brando picture, but al-

The Journeyman and the Apprentice

so because of its educational value to Jack. She thought what better way to introduce him to Shakespeare than through a contemporary film with a bona fide Hollywood movie star of Brando's caliber.

She was making it her mission to acquaint him with some culture and learning, and she was secretly hoping that when she went back to City College for spring semester, maybe Jack would want to take a night class with her. She thought he was really smart, and by just working and not going to school, he wasn't living up to his full potential.

He'd finished reading *Cannery Row*, and she'd bought him a paperback copy of *The Adventures of Huckleberry Finn*. When she first gave it to him, he dismissed it as some kind of a kid's book, but with her assurance that it wasn't, he started reading, and he was finding that he liked it, and he could see that it was clearly not a kid's book, but a work of "adult fiction," whatever that might mean. It was a term he heard her use to describe it and other books she told him about. As he read and got into the adventure, she started to ask him questions, and she pointed out things she wanted him to look for. Sometimes he read late into the night, engrossed in the story, and other times he'd set the book aside and think about Carmela. She'd think about him, too, from time to time, but she knew she couldn't think too seriously because she had other goals. She was determined to go to college, and she wasn't going to let anything or anybody stand in the way of that goal.

Jack had won Teresa over at Thanksgiving, but any esteem she might have cultivated for him since then was eroding because she wasn't seeing him at Mass every Sunday. Since Carmela had told her that he was a Catholic, she was bothered by the fact that he was missing Mass so much. It was a mortal sin after all. Her earlier mistrust of him was returning; however, it was tempered by her mother's and her daughter's liking him. Teresa was certainly outnumbered by the other members of her family. She knew Carlos liked him because he talked about Jack all the time: how he did good flat tops, how he knew how to talk to and handle the customers, how he'd built a following in two months and increased Carlos' business in the process, and how likeable he was. In spite of all these things, Teresa still felt uneasy about him and his attentions to Carmela, and she was especially concerned that Carmela might forget about her studies and going to college to get seriously involved with him.

154

The Journeyman and the Apprentice

They saw *Julius Caesar* downtown at the Los Angeles theater on Monday night, five days before Christmas. After the show they strolled down Broadway, looking in the windows at the shop displays. In the jewelry stores, most of the good stuff had been removed, but a few places had some inexpensive items still on display. When they stopped in front of one, they gazed in at some rings lined up on gray velvet fingers.

"Oh, look at that beautiful purple stone," Carmela said, pointing at an amethyst.

"Wow. Pretty bitchin', huh?"

"Yes. I wonder how much it costs."

Jack just nodded and didn't say a word. He had it in his head that he'd buy it for her. It would make a good Christmas present. He'd already gotten her a leather brief case for her school books. He planned to give it to her on Christmas day. The only other people he'd shopped for so far were David's parents. He'd gotten Señor Pacheco a box of Dutch Masters panetellas and his wife a basket filled with yarn for her knitting. He really wasn't thinking of getting anything for anybody else. Just Carmela.

The next day on his lunch hour, he drove down to the jewelry store and gave the jeweler some money to hold the ring for him. That night he made a date with Carmela for Friday afternoon, Christmas Eve. She got off work at noon and he picked her up and took her to the jewelry store. When they got there, and she could see what he was up to, she became effusive. She saw the ring on display in the window with a little tag on it that said, "Sold," and she began to cry. The jeweler was a stubby little man with a bald head and rimless glasses. He got the ring out of the window, removed the tag, and presented it to Jack to put on Carmela's finger. It seemed to fit just right, so there was no need to size it. Jack paid the jeweler the balance, and the jeweler gave him the gray velvet box the ring came in.

They went back to the shop and showed it to Carlos. Teresa wasn't home yet, but she would be soon. She was also getting off early for the holiday. In the meantime Jack went back to work, and Carmela took a walk down to Gloria's house to show her the ring. When she left there, she went to the Gateway to meet Teresa when she got off. Teresa wasn't as happy about Jack's Christmas gift as Carmela was. Indeed, she wasn't happy at all.

"So, does this mean you're engagedt now?" Teresa said as they walked up Cypress

The Journeyman and the Apprentice

Avenue. "Are you giveen up on goeen to college?"

"No, Mamá," Carmela replied, evenly, though Teresa sensed the irritation in her voice.

"You don't have to get all enojado."

"I'm not getting angry. It's not a diamond; it's an amethyst. It's only a Christmas present."

They stopped at Señora Guevara's house, and she joined them walking back to the Rángel's.

Jack didn't say anything when they got to the shop. He could tell that Teresa was perturbed, and he thought if he said anything, she would only be more upset. Then he thought he might lighten up her anger if he bought her and Carlos Christmas presents, too. What was he thinking, not getting them *and* Señora Guevara presents? He still had time to get her a basket of yarn like he'd done for David's mother, and as far as Carlos was concerned, a couple six packs of Eastside would do the trick. He'd get the beer at Enrique's place. That way he'd be giving the grocer a present, too, a present of cash. He'd have to figure something out for Señora Guevara.

The three ladies went upstairs into the kitchen and started making tamales.

Jerome Arthur

When the two barbers finished cutting hair for the day, Jack didn't go upstairs with Carlos. Instead he took off first to Enrique's and picked up the beer. He put it in his back seat and drove to the store where he'd gotten the yarn for Señora Pacheco. He got there just in time, before the place closed for the holiday. The lady there gift-wrapped Teresa's yarn for him. On his way back to the Rángels, he saw a religious store where a woman was turning the open sign around to the closed side. He pulled up to the curb and went over to the door and knocked softly on one of the nine lights.

"'Scuse me, Ma'm," he said as she turned and came back to the door. "Sorry to bother you late like this, but I really got'a get my future grandmother-in-law a Christmas present. I know you wan'a get home with your family, and I think you should...."

She held up a hand and said, "Please come in. I'll be happy to help you."

As she pulled the door open he saw a ten-by-twelve framed picture of the Holy Family on the back wall. He walked straight to it and said,

"This here looks pretty good. How much is it?"

"That's seven-ninety-five plus tax."

158

The Journeyman and the Apprentice

"Could you gift-wrap it for me?"

"Absolutely."

And so he finished his Christmas shopping. He stuffed everything but the beer in a pillowcase that looked like a Santa Claus bag.

It was still early, so he drove back over to Carmela's house and delivered the bag of presents. Teresa came out of the hallway and put more presents under the tree, and since the one Jack gave Carlos wasn't gift-wrapped, Carlos broke open a couple beers, and the two men drank them as the women had coffee. As Señora Guevara continued to work on the tamales, the others sat in the living room and looked out the picture window at the view of Elysian Park across the train yard on the other side of the river. Lights twinkled in Toonerville, the neighborhood on Riverside Drive.

"I haven't seen you at Mass lately, Jack," Teresa said.

"Yeah, I ain't missin'. I j'st been goin' to Saint Mary's with the Pachecos. Speaking of Mass, me 'n' Carmela're goin' to midnight Mass down Saint Vibianna's Cathedral tonight. How 'bout you and Carlos and your mother comin' along?"

She was taken aback by this invitation.

"Since I'm not workeen late tonight, I'm goeen to bedt early."

Teresa knew she and Carlos would be sound asleep in another couple hours. She went into the kitchen to ask her mother.

"¿Quieres ir con Jack y Carmela a la misa de la media noche?" she said.

"Sí."

"Mamá says she'd like to go," Teresa said, coming back into the living room.

"Great. We'll take her."

As if sensing that Jack wanted to talk to Teresa alone, Carlos took Carmela outside to look at the view.

"Yuh know," Jack said, "when you guys were in the shop earlier, you were acting like you were mad at me. That 'cause I gave Carmela the ring?"

"Well, yes. I'm just worriedt that Carmela won't get her college education."

"Don't worry about it. Not only do I not wan'a see her drop out; I wan'a see her go full-time and finish. Get her degree."

"You sure about that?"

"Absolutely. She's even getting me interested in goin'."

"Well, I'm sure gladt to hear that. The ring you gave her got me a little worriedt."

160

The Journeyman and the Apprentice

"It's only a Christmas present."

After a while Carlos and Carmela came back in the house. At ten o'clock Teresa and Carlos went to bed, and Señora Guevara joined Jack and Carmela in the living room where they talked and listened to yuletide festivities on the radio.

At eleven-thirty they got into the car and headed down to the cathedral for midnight Mass. The Cardinal himself was saying the Mass. He gave a long sermon, and the pomp and circumstance extended the ceremony. It ended at five after one, and a standing-room-only crowd spilled out onto the sidewalk. Jack, Carmela and Señora Guevara got into the car and headed back to Cypress Park. The early morning was chilly and quiet. Jack would like to have gone someplace to eat, but because it was Christmas, restaurants that were usually open at that hour of the morning were closed, so he took Señora Guevara to her house and drove Carmela home.

They got there by one forty-five and didn't go up right away. Rather, they sat in the car smooching. The cold finally got to them, so they reluctantly got out of the steamy car and went upstairs. She invited him inside, offering him a cup of hot chocolate and a tamale. She moved quietly around the kitchen, not wanting to wake her parents. After she got the two cups ready, they moved into the dining room and sat down. As they whispered and sipped their hot chocolate, Teresa came out of her bedroom, sleep still heavy on her eyes. She was wrapped in a pink terry cloth robe.

"I'm sorry, Mamá. Did we wake you?"

"Not really. I was awake before you came home, and when I heardt you talkeen, I decidedt to come out and join you."

She took a carton from the refrigerator and poured herself a glass of eggnog. She put a tamale on a plate and sat down at the table. Just then the bedroom door squeaked open, and Carlos came out. He also fixed himself a glass of eggnog and a tamale and sat down.

"You know, since we're all awake and it *is* Christmas, we migh's well open our presents," Carlos said.

"That's a great idea," Carmela seconded.

"But what about Mamá," Teresa said. "She shouldt be here with us, don't you think?"

"How about if we just open the presents we gave each other, and then tomorrow we open the rest when your mother's here."

"I guess it wouldt be all right," Teresa said.

162

The Journeyman and the Apprentice

"Guess I'll go home and get me some shut-eye," Jack said after they'd each opened a present. "What time you guys goin' to Mass in the morning?"

"Nine o'clock," Carlos said.

"So what time should I come over?"

"Anytime after ten'd be okay."

"Great. I'll go by the church and bring you guys home. Okay?"

"That'd be good."

He walked his empty hot chocolate mug over to the sink and set it down on the drain board. Carmela went out the door with him. He hugged and kissed her and descended the stairs to his car. As soon as he walked through his front door, he took his clothes off and went straight to bed and slept till eight-thirty.

Eleven

Christmas morning was crisp and sunny. Jack picked up Carlos and Teresa at the church at ten to ten. Then he drove to Señora Guevara's house and picked her up. When they got to Carlos' house, Carmela was preparing a breakfast of huevos rancheros. Everybody sat down at the table.

Jack spent the next half-hour practicing his Spanish with Señora Guevara over breakfast. Carmela watched and listened, and her admiration for Jack grew. Her grandmother was also impressed and charmed. Even Teresa was more impressed with Jack than she'd ever been before.

After breakfast they all gathered around the tree and passed out presents. Carmela gave Jack a hardbound copy of Henry James's *The American*. She'd signed it on the inside front cover with a Christmas greeting and words of encouragement, telling him to take his time and

The Journeyman and the Apprentice

enjoy the story. Señora Guevara also gave him a book, in Spanish, a collection of poems written by authors from México and Central America. Jack in turn gave Señora Guevara the picture of the Holy Family, and he gave Carmela a beautiful brown leather briefcase.

Carlos handed him an envelope with his name on it. When he opened it, he found a card with a crisp, new twenty-dollar bill inside. The inscription on the card said simply, "Here's a Christmas bonus for you, Jack," and it was signed first by Carlos and Teresa. He could tell from the handwriting that Teresa had written it. It sounded like Carlos had dictated the message to her, and she transcribed it onto the card in her smooth, flowing script. Her handwriting was much neater and more decorative than Carlos' hurried, illegible scrawl. They all liked the gifts Jack had gotten them. Carmela really liked the briefcase.

"You shouldn't have," she said when he took it out of the bag and handed it to her.

"Couldn't help it," he said. "I thought it'd be perfect for when yuh start school full-time. Look here, it's got different compartments for different size books, and look at these slots for your pens and pencils. There's a leather shoulder strap right here in this compartment. It hooks onto these rings."

After he'd shown her the features, he sat back and let her look it over. He stole a glance at Teresa to see if he could tell if she caught his reference to Carmela's going to City full-time (he wasn't aware yet that Carlos was about to tell her that she could), but he couldn't tell much from Teresa's expression, only that she seemed reasonably happy and content, and was having a very merry Christmas. After the presents were opened, and the living room was strewn with wrapping paper and curly ribbons, Carlos dropped the surprise bombshell.

"Now comes the big present for you, honey. Jack and me've been doin' a good business lately, so I think it's about time you gave notice at the insurance company and started taking a full load at City."

"Oh, Papá! Do you really mean it?"

"Absolutely. Wouldn't've said it if I didn't."

She crossed the room and gave her father a big hug and a kiss on the cheek. After that they talked and listened to Christmas music on the radio as the ladies straightened up the living room.

The Journeyman and the Apprentice

At a little after noon, Jack and Carmela got into the car and drove over to Raul's house. From there they went to pick up Gloria and then to Boyle Heights to call on the Pachecos.

"You guys get a lota' cool stuff for Christmas?" Jack asked Raul and Gloria, as they cruised through Five Points onto Daly Street.

"I got this Pendleton and these khakis," Raul said, pointing to the clothes he was wearing.

"Mamá gave me this sweater."

Gloria was wearing a pink cashmere.

"My grandmother gave Jack a collection of poems all in Spanish. Pretty good, huh?"

"Can you readt Spanish?" Gloria asked.

"You guys're go'n'a have to help me out."

"I told her you probably don't read Spanish well enough to get through it," said Carmela, "but she liked it and you so much, she got it for you anyway."

"Hey, I like her, too, and I'm glad she likes me. Makes up for your mom. Sometimes I don't think she likes me."

"What do you mean? Mamá likes you all right. She just worries about me and my future. She certainly has her prejudices, but she's only wary of you because she's afraid I might do

167

something foolish like drop out of college and run off somewhere with you. But now everybody knows that's not going to happen." At this point, she looked at Gloria and said, "Papá gave me the best present of all. He said I can quit my job and go to school."

"That's great!" Gloria said.

"Yeah. Now Teresa don't have to worry if I'm go'n'a sneak off with you." Jack said.

"Like I said she has her prejudices, and one of them is about religion. She still isn't sure how good a Catholic you are. I think she's gotten over the ethnic part of it; your Spanish has won her over. That's definitely your biggest asset with Grandma. She loves how you speak Spanish."

At one-thirty they were on the concrete path that led to the Pacheco's front porch. As they'd done on Thanksgiving, Mister and Missus Pacheco and Margarita came out of the house to greet the four young people as they approached.

"Feliz Navidad, mijito," Señora Pacheco said to Jack as she hugged him. Then she turned to Carmela and the others with the same greeting, holding her hands out to them.

"¿Donde está David?" Jack asked Señor Pacheco.

168

The Journeyman and the Apprentice

"Tiene que trabajar hoy. Perhaps you could go see him when you leave here."

"Sí, es posible," Jack said looking at Carmela and the others.

"Seguramente. We'll go see him at work before we go back to my house," Carmela said, addressing the Pachecos in her flawless Spanish.

Señora Pacheco offered the four young people some tamales. They took places around the dining room table. After they'd eaten, Señor Pacheco took Jack and Raul out to the front porch where he offered the younger men cigars from the box Jack had given him for Christmas and lit a match to the three. The ladies picked up the dishes from the table and stacked them on the drain board next to the kitchen sink. They went into the living room and sat down, but not for long. It was too nice a day to stay cooped up inside, so after a short while they joined the men on the porch. They sat on wicker furniture in the low shade of the California bungalow's porch and talked for about an hour. When visiting families from around the neighborhood passed by on the sidewalk, they'd exchange Christmas greetings, "Feliz Navidad."

At three o'clock Jack and his friends left to go visit David at the supermarket where he worked. Missus Pacheco was disappointed that

169

they were leaving, but she was happy to have seen them for as long as she had. She and her husband accompanied them down to the car and stood at the curb until they pulled away, waving to them as they left.

Jack turned onto Third Street and drove through Belvedere until he hit Beverly Boulevard. The Ralph's store was two blocks from Third and Beverly. He was surprised to find so many cars in the parking lot, and when he saw the crowd inside the store, he was astonished at how busy it was. David was bagging groceries at one of the check stands. As the two couples walked toward him, he looked up from his work.

"What's hopponeen, eh?" he said with a smile. He continued putting the groceries into the bag in front of him. "Stick around. I get a break when I finish this one. We could hang out for ten minutes."

"Okay," Jack said. "Meet yuh outside."

They went out front and waited for David in the parking lot. The person he was helping was a woman by herself, and she'd bought three shopping bags of groceries and a twenty-pound bag of dog food. David put the bags into a shopping cart, the dog food underneath, and started wheeling it out to her car. After he put

170

The Journeyman and the Apprentice

the bags into the back seat of the car, he pushed the cart back to the front of the store.

"I'll be right back," he said to the group as he passed them.

He went in and punched his timecard. When he came back out, the five of them walked past the sorry collection of unsold Christmas trees and on down the street.

"You guys go over my folks's house before you came here?"

"Yeah. Had a good time. Your folks're so cool. How come you had'a work today?"

"It's how they scheduledt me. I've known about it since the beginneen of the month."

"Thought you were supposed to get promoted to checker."

"Maybe by New Years. Mostly Judios workeen here. It's hard if you ain't a Judio. Only a couple other Méxicanos, and they're no better off'n me. You know how that works."

"Yeah."

"So, what're you guys doeen?"

"Headin' back over Cypress. Maybe take a detour up Griffith Park. Check out the sunset."

"Sounds bonaroo. Nice day for it, eh. I got'a work till six. Sun'll be down by then. Oh, well."

Jerome Arthur

"We're barely go'n'a make it."

They'd turned around and headed back to the store. When David's break ended, he left the group in the parking lot and went back to work. They went up into the Griffith Park hills. The sky was crystal clear as they watched the sun make its descent over Sunset Boulevard. When the evening sky grew dark, the cold forced them to put jackets on. Winter cold was the price they paid for clear skies.

When they got back to Carmela's house, Carlos and Teresa were alone. Shortly after the young people had gone to Boyle Heights, Carlos and Teresa received four more guests. Señora Guevara was still there when Enrique and María Elena Contreras showed up. Then Carlos' cousin, Julio, who had a trucking company in Long Beach, made an appearance. He and his wife stayed for a couple of hours hoping to meet Jack, but they didn't want to drive back to Long Beach after dark, so they left for home well before sunset. Jack had heard about Julio from Carlos and was disappointed at having missed him.

"Yeah, he was disappointed, too," Carlos said. "Maybe in spring we could go down there on a Monday, catch him at work. Get him to take us out to lunch."

172

The Journeyman and the Apprentice

"Sounds like a plan."

Jack and Carmela took Gloria and Raul home at eight o'clock, and then went back to her house. He and Carlos sat by the living room window talking and looking at the view. Carmela played Christmas songs on the piano. Teresa sat next to her on the piano bench. It was the best Christmas Jack had ever had. At eight o'clock they had some of Señora Guevara's tamales.

"Wha'da yuh say we start remodeling the shop after the first of the year?" Carlos said as they ate. "Waiting chairs're all done. I'm go'n'a try to get those new barber chairs delivered. The ones I ordered from Lou. Paint the place. Put new linoleum down."

"Hey, I'm game."

"We could start next Monday after New Years."

"No problem."

Jack got up to leave and told them he'd see them at Mass in the morning. Then Carmela accompanied him out the door and down to his car. They stepped into the shadow on the other side of the barber shop where Carmela knew Teresa couldn't see them, if she happened to be looking, and they hugged and kissed in the cold winter night. They separated only because the

173

hot kisses were no match for the cold winter chill. He drove off in the late Christmas quiet, and she hurried up the stairs to the warmth of the house.

Twelve

The shop remained busy through the holidays. On Monday the third of January, Jack pulled up in front at nine o'clock. Carlos came down from the house and got in the car.

"Go down the barber supply first," he said.

"Cool."

They took the Arroyo Seco Parkway into downtown to Freeman Barber Supply. The chairs Carlos had picked out over a month ago from a brochure Lou had shown him were chrome and muted yellow porcelain with brown leather cushions and backs. They were Paidars, the same brand and similar in style to the ones he was getting rid of, not like the new barrel-style barber chairs that were coming into fashion.

When they entered the store, to the right of the front door was a full display of a one chair barber shop: a chair sitting in front of a

Belvadere shampoo bowl that hung on a two-cabinet Formica backbar with built-in mirrors. Straight ahead of them about twenty feet away, a bald guy behind a glass display case was talking on the telephone.

"I think that's the chair I ordered right there," Carlos said, going over to it. He walked around it and looked it over. Then he pumped it up a few pumps, held the pump forward, let it back down. He sat in it and turned it so that he was facing the mirror. "Yeah, this is it. Wha'da yuh think?"

Jack pumped it once to release the brake, turned it to look at Carlos' taper in the mirror. He stood behind him and pantomimed a flat top. Just as he was about to tell Carlos that he liked it, the guy with the bald head joined them in the mock shop.

"Help you gents?"

"Yeah. I'm Carlos Rángel. My shop's up in Cypress Park. Last month I put in an order with Lou for a couple new chairs just like this one. Wan'a go 'head on and get 'em delivered. Get my old ones outa' there."

"Okeedoke. Let's take a look at the invoices," he said and started back toward his counter. The two barbers were right behind him. On the counter was a flat box with a stack of

176

The Journeyman and the Apprentice

invoices in it which he started thumbing through. "Yeah, here it is," he said when he found the order blank Lou had filled out in mid November. "Yuh go'n'a pay the balance now?"

"Well, actually I can give yuh a hundred and fifty bucks right now and another fifty when the chairs are delivered. Then I'll pay yuh fifty a month till they're paid off, and you take my old chairs off my hands. That's the deal Lou gave me."

"Looks about right according to the way he wrote it up here. When yuh want the chairs?"

"Soon as yuh can bring 'em. Anytime this week'd be fine."

"We got 'em in last week. Wan'a take a look? They're in back. We can get 'em to yuh by early Wednesday afternoon right after lunch. That be all right?" the bald guy said after they'd looked at the chairs.

"Perfect."

They drove back out Figueroa to the Benjamin Moore paint store and picked up a couple gallons of a soft, eggshell-white latex, some brushes, and a roller with an extension. Back at the shop, they moved the furniture to the center of the room. Then they took the two mirrors off the wall opposite the chairs. They spread one of the old sheets Teresa had given

177

him over the furniture and thumb-tacked the other two above the backbar mirrors and draped it over the backbars. With both of them painting, they finished the job in a couple of hours. As Carlos looked at the old asphalt tile floor, now spattered with paint, he thought he should get the new linoleum right away. There was still time to go to Sears in Glendale and pick it up, so that's what they did. He'd keep the shop closed tomorrow, and they'd do that job in the morning.

* * *

First thing Tuesday morning, Carlos was moving the furniture out onto the sidewalk. Jack showed up shortly after and got busy helping him. When it was all moved out, they started on the floor. They got down on their hands and knees and scraped the paint speckles with putty knives.

Despite the cold, the day was sunny enough to warm and soften the linoleum. They unrolled it slowly, one section at a time, and it didn't crack. Once they had it spread out on the sidewalk in the sun, Carlos ran up the steps to the patio at the rear of the house where he had a few two-by-fours stored. He grabbed a couple

178

The Journeyman and the Apprentice

and went back down to put them at opposite ends of the linoleum where it had been rolled up. The two guys stood on them as the sun warmed the vinyl, making it supple. Then, leaving the two-by-fours where they were, they went back into the shop and swept and vacuumed the floor. The last thing Carlos did was give it a good damp-mopping.

When they checked on the new flooring material again, it was soft and pliable. They took it back into the shop and marked and cut it. Carlos had turned the heat on early. It was warm enough to keep the linoleum flexible. After they cut it, they rolled it up and started to spread the mastic. As they unrolled the vinyl over the resin, Carlos continued to spread mastic, and Jack got to his feet from time to time and skated on his leather-sole shoes over the newly laid linoleum, trying to flatten out the air pockets. He punctured the ones that wouldn't flatten with a finishing nail. When the mastic was all spread and the linoleum laid, they stood back and looked at their handiwork.

"Looks pretty good," Carlos said.

"Hundred percent improvement."

By now it was time for lunch, so the two men washed their hands and went upstairs. They took chairs opposite each other at the dining

179

room table. Teresa fixed chile verde burritos, and as the men ate, she disappeared into the bedroom to get ready for work. She came back into the kitchen dressed for work in a skirt and blouse, and a thigh-length blue and white Gateway smock with her first name stitched in above the breast pocket. She sat down at the table and ate with the others.

"I'm goeen to work now," she said to Carlos, getting up from the table and taking her plate into the kitchen. "See you at dinner time."

"Okay," he said without getting out of his seat. "Thanks for lunch."

He waved as she turned and headed toward the door.

"Wan'a beer, eh?" Carlos said to Jack.

"Sounds good."

He got up, went to the refrigerator and came back with the two bottles and a church key. They put their dishes in the sink and took their beers back down to the shop.

"Looking sharp."

"You bet," Jack said.

They drank their beers and admired their handiwork. Then they started to nail the baseboard molding on. When they finished doing that, they very carefully moved the furniture back into the shop. They probably should have

180

The Journeyman and the Apprentice
waited a little longer for the mastic to harden,
but Carlos didn't want to leave his furniture outside any longer, so they cleared everything from
the sidewalk and put it in its place. Then they
put the finishing touches on the place.

"We ought'a get another shampoo bowl
and put the chairs in front of 'em instead of in
front of the cabinets," said Jack. "Like the setup
they had at the barber supply. That way when
we wan'a do a shampoo, alls we got'a do is re-
cline 'em back insteada' puttin' 'em on a stool
face-first in the sink. I wan'a eventually start
doin' shampoos with every cut, like the way
beauticians and upscale barbers do. You know
the Mullin and Bluett building down Sixth and
Broadway?"

"Yeah?"

"They got a barber shop on the second
floor, and that's the way they do it. Yuh ought'a
see how nice the cuts come out when yuh do it
like that."

"Where exactly you wan'a put the
chairs?" Carlos asked.

"C'm'ere, I'll show yuh."

Trying to take it easy on the new floor
again, they very carefully moved Carlos' chair
in front of the one sink they had, and Jack sat
him down and reclined him back into the bowl.

"Yeah, I see what yuh mean. But don't the sink get in your way when you're cutting the guy's hair?"

"Not if yuh turn your chair sideways so when you're behind it, you're standing next to your backbar. Also, yuh get natural light from the window on your work."

As he was saying it, he was turning the chair to the position he was describing.

"Good idea. And if it don't work out, we can always change it back to the way it was."

They moved the chair back in front of the cabinet, did the last bit of tidying up, and went upstairs, leaving the transom light over the door open to air the place out. They sat at the dining room table and had another beer.

"What're yuh doing for dinner tonight?" Carlos asked Jack as he was getting up to leave. It was three o'clock.

"I ain't got no plans other than pickin' Carmela up. 'Member it *is* Tuesday. Her first day back at school after Christmas vacation."

"Oh yeah, that's right. I was go'n'a say come on over here for dinner, but Carmela ain't even go'n'a be here."

"I think I'll take her over Tommy's after her class. You guys'll prob'ly be in bed by the time we get home. The class don't end till ten.

182

The Journeyman and the Apprentice

We probably won't get outa' Tommy's till at least eleven."

"Yeah, well don't keep her out too late. 'Member, her mother still ain't a hundred percent on you, yet. She's making progress, and I'd hate see that end."

"Don't worry. I know how it is. I also don't wan'a keep her out too late 'cause she's got'a be up early in the morning to go to work."

By the time Jack left, he was tired, so when he got home, he took a nap. He had five hours before he had to pick up Carmela. He slept till almost seven o'clock. When he got up, he took a shower and then read till nine. He got her home, as he'd told Carlos, at eleven-thirty.

Thirteen

Though it didn't happen until almost seven o'clock in winter, daybreak came too early for both Jack and Carlos on that cold January morning. They'd both worked hard the past two days, a lot of hands-and-knees stuff, and they were tired. Also, Carlos worried and fretted over whether business would justify the remodel.

...now i got'a pay *for everything, so i hope the customers start lining up...carmela gave her notice monday...won't be having that income no more....*

Since he was so anxious to get into his new shop, he went down to it as soon as Carmela left for work. It smelled of fresh paint and new linoleum. He closed the transom and turned the heat on. As he waited while the place heated up, he stood back and looked it over: the four newly upholstered waiting chairs, the magazines and comic books stacked neatly on the table, the cash register and its stand with its little com-

The Journeyman and the Apprentice

partment underneath, where he kept back issues of *Esquire* and *Down Beat*. Carlos spent some time moving things around and then stepping back to see how it looked.

He heard a vehicle pull up out in front, and when he turned to look, he was surprised to see Lou behind the wheel of his Freeman Barber Supply van.

...híjola...what's he doing here...ain't supposed to show up till after lunch....

Jack pulled up behind the van.

"I wasn't expecting you this early," Carlos said. "Ain't go'n'a have the dough till after noon."

"Hmph. Maybe I should check with Jim at the store. Pretty sure it's go'n'a be okay, though."

They went inside and gathered around the pay phone next to the cash register. Lou fished a nickel out of his pocket and put it in the slot. He dialed the number and waited for an answer.

"Jim? Lou here. These chairs I'm delivering out here on Cypress Avenue. Carlos says he wasn't expecting 'em till this afternoon. Says he ain't got the dough right now." Pause while he listened to the voice on the other end. "Uh, huh. Okay. So you wan'a talk to 'im? Here he is." He offered the receiver to Carlos.

"Hello, this is Carlos Rángel."

"Yeah, Carlos. This is Jim Johnson." Carlos recognized the voice of the man with the bald head, whom he'd spoken to on Monday.

"Wha'da yuh want me to do?"

"Look, why don't you just go ahead and take the chairs, and you can send me a check later. Lou's already there. He can just go ahead and leave 'em and pick up your old ones. That sound okay to you?"

"Yeah, sure. Tell yuh what I'm go'n'a do. I'll come down to your store on Monday and pay yuh the cash in person. And when I do, I'm go'n'a order a new shampoo bowl like the one I got."

"That'll be fine. We have some in stock. I think we can match it up."

"Says he wants yuh to leave 'em," Carlos said to Lou after he hung up.

"Right."

He went out to the van and got a hand truck with a canvas strap and wheeled it into the shop. A few minutes later, the two old chairs were sitting on the sidewalk out front. By nine o'clock opening time, the replacements were installed, and the van was driving away. The

186

The Journeyman and the Apprentice

two barbers now stood back by the front door and looked the place over. Then they walked to the back of the shop and looked from that angle. It was a brand-new barber shop.

"Customers're go'n'a start comin' in now. This is go'n'a be one of the hottest little shops around," Jack said over his shoulder to Carlos as he went to the utility cabinet in the alcove for Windex to clean the backbar mirrors and the ones on the wall opposite the chairs and backbars.

Carlos went out onto the sidewalk to look in at the place through the front window. Jack looked over to see his smile of approval for the job they'd done. At nine-twenty Carlos' first customer came in and sat in the new leather-smelling chair. Jack looked at the empty wall space and thought it needed some color.

There were two large calendars hanging side by side in the rest room, a 1954 and a '55. Lou had given them to Carlos the last two Christmases. The Freeman Barber Supply logo separated the pictures on top from the stack of twelve sheets of paper for each month stapled to the bottom. The two pictures were about a foot square. The older one was a Mojave Desert sunset, the other a Pacific sunset. None of the months was torn off the 'fifty-four. It looked

187

like Carlos had abandoned it as soon as he had gotten it.

Jack took both calendars out into the shop. He cut the picture off the 'fifty-four calendar and threw the unused calendar into the trash. Then he dug out some thumb tacks and tacked it to the wall on one side of the cash register. As he was hanging the 'fifty-five calendar on the other side, a customer came in and put him to work. It was the first time in the new year that the new shop had both of its chairs going at once. Carlos' barber shop was back in business.

*   *   *

The two barbers had a busy first day of the New Year. The customers all said how good the shop looked. They were so busy that Carlos had not found time to get over to Contreras' store. He barely found time to get upstairs for lunch. Jack made time to go downtown and take Carmela out to lunch.

"You didn't really tell me last night how your boss took it when you told 'im you're quittin'?"

"He wasn't too happy about it. He offered me a raise to stay."

188

The Journeyman and the Apprentice

"Yeah, right!"

Jack's sarcasm was obvious.

"He was very nice. He understood why I was leaving, and he wished me luck in school."

"Just so you don't worry about whether your parents'll miss your income, we had a real busy morning in the shop. I left your dad with a shop full of customers, and I think it's go'n'a be like that from now on."

It had been so busy, in fact, that Jack didn't want to leave Carlos alone for too long, so he and Carmela finished their lunches, and he got back to the shop an hour and fifteen minutes after he'd left. It was as busy in the afternoon as it had been in the morning. The shop grossed sixty dollars on the first day after reopening. For the first time since Jack came to work for him, Carlos was confident that he could make enough money to support his family and send his daughter to college full-time. Finally, he was thinking he didn't have to worry about the business anymore. It was taking care of itself. But some things still bothered him, like his indebtedness to the barber supply.

Carlos and Jack kept busy through the rest of the week. When Monday came, Jack drove Carlos to Freeman, and Carlos paid Jim his money. Jim showed him the sinks he had in

189

stock, and luckily, there was one that matched the one he had. In addition, Jack paid cash and got a receipt for forty-eight white terry-cloth shampoo towels, and a gallon and two quart-size with pumps of Stephan's shampoo. He was on a roll.

"We'll talk some more about this stuff after we get the sink hung," he said.

On the way back to the shop, Jack took a detour to a stationary store in Highland Park. Carlos looked doubtful as Jack picked up a couple of 1955 Day-at-a-Glance appointment books, two number-two pencils, and two pink erasers. He also bought a pencil sharpener and a Scripto ballpoint. He got it all for less than three dollars.

If he learned anything from his time aboard ship, he learned that when you've got a captive audience (and he was confident that his and Carlos' clientele was locked in), scheduling appointments is the best way to go. He'd told his chief that if the guys had appointments, they wouldn't be wasting a lot of time hanging around the barber shop waiting for a haircut. The supply officer in charge of ship's service also thought that was a good idea, so both he and the chief told Jack to go ahead and set it up.

190

The Journeyman and the Apprentice

Now Jack wanted to do the same with Carlos' shop.

"Check it out," he said, when they got back. "One for you, one for me. We're go'n'a start scheduling appointments. Know what you're go'n'a do now?"

"No. What?"

"Call the phone company and get 'em to exchange this pay phone for a regular business line."

Jack walked to the bi-level cabinet opposite the barber chairs next to the pay phone. He eyeballed the area around the phone, and then turned and looked at the backbar. Pointing to a spot on his own backbar next to Carlos' sink, he said,

"You can put the phone right here. We can both get to it easy, and we can put our appointment books and pencils on our backbars. Starting tomorrow we'll write people's names in the books as they come in, and when we're done with their haircuts, we'll give 'em one a' your business cards. Tell 'em to call and make an appointment next time."

"Yuh think yuh might be moving a little fast here? What if the customers don't wan'a make appointments?"

Jerome Arthur

"It ain't up to them. It's up to us. We make our own schedules around here. We're in charge. Not them."

"Yuh know, I think you're right. Hell with it. Let's do it."

Then they got busy installing the new shampoo bowl on the other side of Jack's back-bar. Luckily the guy who'd built the shop had planned on a second sink. There were hot and cold shutoff valves and a capped-off waste pipe in the wall. All they had to do was get the pea-trap and the water pipes from the hardware store and hang the sink. But as jobs like that often go, especially for barbers who aren't plumbers, they didn't finish until mid afternoon. They moved the chairs so they lined up with the shampoo bowls, and they were ready to go. They were set to start doing shampoos with every haircut the next morning.

"Okay. Now, here's what we're go'n'a do with the haircuts. This is why I got those towels, and the shampoo. My dad used to do it like this. It's the way they do it in Canada. We're go'n'a include a shampoo with all our haircuts. And to get the customers to try it, we're go'n'a offer it to 'em the first time for what we're chargin' 'em now for just a haircut, a buck twenty-five, but their next haircut, with

192

The Journeyman and the Apprentice

the shampoo, is go'n'a cost 'em three bucks, and that's what we'll be chargin' till the next time we raise the price."

"I hope you know what you're doin'. These're some big changes."

"Let's start the new year out right. Have I steered you wrong so far? First time I talked to yuh, yuh said there wasn't enough for two barbers, and I told yuh not to worry about it. And sure enough, first four days of the year, could've used three barbers."

"Can't argue with that."

After they folded the towels and made room for them in their cabinets, they stood back and looked at the place. Carlos couldn't help but feel some pride in their accomplishment.

"I'm goin' upstairs, get us a couple beers. Be right back."

They sat in their new barber chairs and sipped their beers and admired the shop.

"Yuh wan'a come back for dinner. I'm sure the ladies'd like for yuh to come. Wha'da yuh say?"

"Sure."

With that, they closed up the shop and went their separate ways. Jack got back at quarter after six. After dinner Teresa went back to work. Carmela went to her room to study for the final in her class. Jack went home, and Carlos went down to the shop and played his sax until it was time to go get Teresa. He even started composing a tune.

When Carlos got to the Gateway to walk Teresa home, she had a poster someone at work had given her. It was a copy of a painting of a matador, straight-legged, cape laid across the sword, doing a pass. The bull had his head raised.

"Thought you couldt use this in the shop," she said. "Brighten the place up."

"Let's go put it up right now," he said.

"Go 'headt, mijo. I'm goeen upstairs, sit down and unwind."

Carlos hung the poster on the back wall, so it would be the first thing anybody looking in the window would see. After he finished, he took a moment to look the place over again. He really liked what he saw.

"How's the poster look?" Teresa said as he came in the house. "Looks good. Adds a lota' color."

"How was your day."

"Real good. Wait'll yuh see what we're go'n'a do starting tomorrow."

"Oh no. What are you up to now, Carlitos?"

194

The Journeyman and the Apprentice

She rolled her eyes, half joking, half concerned. She was glad that business was getting better, but she was also somewhat unsettled by how fast things were moving, and the money Carlos was spending on the improvements. He told her how Jack had bought the towels and shampoo and appointment books, and then he explained the new routine to her. Shampoo cuts. By appointment.

"You know, I am worriedt about the money, but this sounds like one of the best things you've done, yet."

"Think so?"

"Sí, mijo."

"I wondered how open to it you were go'n'a be. I can remember when you didn't think too much of Jack."

"That was when I first met him. I was just be-een careful is all. But you and Carmela and Mamá were right from the beginneen. Jack's a goodt boy."

"He's doin' a lota' good things for my shop."

They talked like that for a while longer, and then turned in for the night.

Fourteen

Carlos was getting in the habit of going downstairs early every morning and after hours at night. Now that the shop was such a nice, comfortable space, he didn't mind just sitting there and hanging out. He would relax in his "new shop" as he played his saxophone, which, he found, he was devoting more time to, not less, now that he was busy cutting hair. His music, like his business, was developing a life of its own. Even though he had less time in his daily schedule to work on it, he set aside time at night for his music while Carmela studied and Teresa was at work. He wasn't listening to the radio as much as he used to.

The day after Jack got the towels, shampoo and appointment books, Contreras came out of his store and crossed the street.

"¡Híjola!" he said as he entered. "Your shop's lookeen all to'a madre, ese. You vatos been busy fixeen things up. Think yuh can cut

The Journeyman and the Apprentice

my hair right now? I got María Elena keepeen an eye on the store."

"This is perfect. You could be my first guinea pig for our new routine."

"Wha'da yuh mean?"

"Okay, here's the deal. From now on I'm go'n'a shampoo your hair before I cut it. First time ain't go'n'a cost yuh no more than what yuh already been paying. It's still only a buck and a quarter, but next time it's go'n'a be three bucks. Wan'a try it?"

"You know I ain't goeen nowhere else for my haircut, eh, so cut it however you want."

Before he started, Carlos wrote Enrique's name in his appointment book. He was in the middle of the shampoo when Jack came in followed by a new customer.

"Órale, Enrique !" he said. "You like our new setup, eh?"

"Ye're spoileen me, eh."

As Jack took the customer back to his chair, Enrique was telling Carlos how he and María Elena had gone to the Rose Parade with her brother and his wife who had driven them up there at five in the morning. They took folding chairs, blankets and Thermos bottles filled with hot brandy. When they got there, the party that had started before midnight was still going.

They joined in and kept on until noon when the last float passed them, and their Thermos jugs were empty.

"It was the cheapest New Years I ever hadt, ese," Contreras said. "And it was fun, too, eh. When the paradte endedt, we took the party over Armando's house. Picked up some menudo. Watched the Rose Bowl game on T.V. Madte some more hot brandies. Diden't quit till seven, eight o'clock that night."

Carlos and Jack stayed busy like that all day. Enrique and several others paid full price that first time. Only two people walked out when they were offered a shampoo as part of the haircut. No matter. Both times someone came in right after them. It was another sixty-dollar day for the shop. And what really got both barbers excited was the thought that their grosses would double the next time they saw these same customers.

By the end of the second week of the new year, the shop had grossed over five hundred dollars. Carlos figured it was probably the busiest first two weeks of the year he'd ever had. Even when he and Jonesy were their busiest after the war, he didn't remember it being this busy. Traditionally in barber shops, the two weeks following the Christmas holidays were

198

The Journeyman and the Apprentice

slow. People were short of cash. All that Christmas shopping had taken its toll on their wallets. What was happening now was a whole new experience for Carlos.

Things were looking up for the other members of his family as well. Carmela got registered at City College as a full-time student, and she started classes at the end of the month. On February first, Teresa started the dayshift at the Gateway. On a Monday in mid January Terry Snyder had called her into his office and offered it to her. She punched out at six o'clock and hurried home to tell her family the good news. When she entered the house, Carlos was sitting at the dining room table talking through the kitchen door to Carmela who was making spaghetti and meat sauce for dinner.

"It's finally happenedt!" Teresa said enthusiastically. "Terry Snyder put me on the dayshift. I start the first of February."

"That's great, honey!" Carlos said. "You got the job!"

"I can't believe how nice Terry Snyder has turnedt out."

"I'm glad to see you're finally lightening up on the gavachos. First Jack, now Terry."

"I'm still not completely convinced."

"You've come a long way, Mamá."

199

Jerome Arthur

Teresa went into the bathroom to wash up for dinner. When she returned, a plate of spaghetti was waiting for her. The family ate in silence. When they finished, Carmela started the dishes, and Teresa went to the bathroom to get ready to go back to work. Carlos sat down next to the radio. He thought he'd listen for a few minutes before he went down to the shop to make his own music. He was tuning it when the doorbell rang. It was Jack, and he'd just been at Raul's house and was on his way home when he decided to drop in on them. Carlos turned the radio off as Jack took a seat on the couch, and they talked. Teresa came out of the bathroom and headed back to work. Carmela joined Carlos and Jack in the living room after she finished the dishes. Carlos told Jack about Teresa's move to the dayshift at the Gateway.

"All right! When did she get it?"

"Just today," Carmela said. "Her new boss is turning out to be a good man."

"Wow, sudden changes, huh?"

"No kidding," Carlos said.

"Pretty cool."

"Spring semester starts next Monday," Carmela said. "I can hardly wait. Gloria and I will go on the streetcar together."

"How 'bout I drive yuh?"

The Journeyman and the Apprentice

"We wanted to leave here by eight o'clock. Do you want to get up that early on your day off?"

"No problem. I wake up at six anyway. 'Fact, I'm go'n'a drive yuh every morning, and pick yuh up on Mondays, if that's okay with you."

"You know I don't have class till ten o'clock on Tuesday and Thursday?"

"That's okay. I'll just take yuh in early. You could study in the library till class starts."

"Good idea. And then I can just take the streetcar home. Can Gloria ride along with us? She's only got classes on Monday, Wednesday and Friday."

"Absolutely."

"Oh, goody. Let's go tell her."

"Let's go."

Carlos walked down the steps with them and went into the shop to work on his music.

"Let's walk?" Carmela said.

"Sure. Why not?"

And once they got going, Jack was glad they were walking. That way he could snuggle with her and not worry about keeping his eyes on the road. He put his arm over her shoulder, and she put hers around his waist. A half block past John's barber shop, they stopped and kissed

Jerome Arthur

in the semi darkness between streetlights. Just as they were about to turn the corner at Gloria's street, a customized 'fifty-two Chevy slowed down, and the guy sitting in the shotgun seat sneered out the open window at Jack,

"Chinga tú madre, pinchi cabrón."

Carmela tensed up and hurried Jack around the corner to Gloria's house, but he resisted briefly and then went along when he saw two guys in the front seat and two in the back.

"Don't pay any attention to them," she said.

"Don't worry. I ain't gettin' into nothin' with those guys. Four to one're lousy odds. Now if there was only two of 'em...," he said with a sarcastic inflection, but he wasn't kidding.

He looked over his shoulder as they turned the corner and saw the Chevy's taillights flicker off down Cypress. Martha answered the door and let Jack and Carmela in.

"Is Gloria here?" Carmela asked when they got inside.

"In her room."

They exchanged pleasantries with Señor and Señora Roybal as they passed through the living room. Gloria was listening to Laverne Baker on her record player.

The Journeyman and the Apprentice

"So, what're you guys doeen?" she asked.

"We just came down to tell you that Jack's taking us to school and picking us up on Monday. He's actually taking me every morning, and you can come with us on the days you go."

"How nice. What time is your first class on Monday?"

"English 1B at nine o'clock. Yours?"

"Not till ten, but that's okay. I'll go early with you. I still don't have all my books. While you're in class, I'll go to the bookstore. You have all your books?"

"Only the one for the English class. I've got an hour between English and psychology. I'll get the psych. book then."

"What time are you pickeen us up?" Gloria asked Jack.

"Go'n'a be at Carmela's house at eight o'clock. Shouldn't take us more'n five minutes to get here from there."

"I'll be ready by eight."

That settled, they left Gloria's and walked back to the house. They didn't see any more vatos cruising around looking for trouble. Jack didn't go upstairs with Carmela. He was tired and it was getting late, so he kissed and hugged her and said good night.

Back in her room, Carmela got out her City College catalogue and her schedule of classes and looked through them. She'd had no trouble getting the classes she wanted. She was signed up for fourteen units of English, history, biology and psychology, all classes she needed to fulfill her general education requirements. She looked at her English text before she went to bed.

After he'd left Carmela, Jack headed straight home, or so he thought. He was driving in the slow lane up Figueroa, when he was aware of a car in the left lane driving abreast of him, maintaining his speed. Wondering why the guy wasn't going on ahead, he turned and saw that it was the customized Chevy he'd seen earlier near Gloria's house. One of the guys in the back seat was pointing a zip gun right at him. He stepped on the gas pedal, and as he shot forward, he heard a "pop" and a "zip," and the sound of cracking safety glass right behind him. Glancing over his shoulder, he could see the spider web crack of the rear window on the driver's side. The Chevy pursued him but couldn't keep up because it was so low that it bottomed out anytime it hit the slightest bump

204

The Journeyman and the Apprentice

or pothole. But it kept following him, and that prompted him to head for the police station on York Boulevard instead of home. When he got to within two blocks of the precinct house, the Chevy turned off and disappeared down a side street.

Jack parked on the street in front of the station house and turned his lights off. He sat there for a few minutes, his heart pounding in his chest. After a while, a couple of guys in uniform came out the front door and walked down the steps. They looked like they'd just gotten off duty and were heading home. One of them came around to Jack's side of the car and asked if he could be of any help. Jack's mistrust of the police dated back to his first bust for joyriding.

"No, it's all right. I was just on my way home, and I think some punks were following me, so I pulled up here, just to be on the safe side. I think they took off when they saw where I was goin'."

"Sure everything's okay?" said the cop. "Looks like someone shot your window."

"Yeah. That happened a couple weeks ago when the car was parked. I think some kid with a slingshot did it. Should be safe to go home now, don't yuh think?"

Jerome Arthur

"Okay, but I suggest you get that window fixed."

"I will."

Jack kept a sharp eye out for the punks on his drive from the police station to his house, but he didn't see them again that night. It was almost ten o'clock when he got home, and he was dead tired, so he quickly brushed his teeth and got into bed. He was asleep before his head hit the pillow.

Fifteen

Carlos and Jack remained busy through the week. On Saturday at the end of the day, Raul showed up at the shop and had a beer with the two barbers and Enrique. When the guys finished cleaning up and the beer bottles emptied, Jack and Raul took off and went down to the bar to have a couple more. When they left the bar, they drove over to East L.A. to get burritos at a little tin shack called El Vacilón in Varrio Nuevo.

As Jack approached the taco stand, he could see the customized 'fifty-two Chevy that hassled him last week, parked in the lot.

"I don't believe it," he said to Raul. "'Member I tol' you how my window got busted?"

"Yeah?"

"That's the car they were in."

"No shit."

There were two guys sitting at the counter of the taco stand.

"All right! Better odds now."

Jack pulled his clunker in next to the Chevy, and as he opened his door, he slammed it twice into the passenger-side door of the Chevy putting a four-inch gash in it. When the two punks saw what was happening, they charged, one guy about six feet in front of the other, right at Jack.

"What choo doeen, pende..."

That was all the guy could get out. Jack was dancing on the balls of his feet, fists clenched. He stepped to the side and delivered a hard-right hook to the side of the guy's face, sending him up against the shotgun-side door of the Chevy. His head slammed so hard against the window that it broke. Then he slumped to the ground, out cold.

"We're even, cabrón," Jack said in as calm and cool a voice as he could use.

Raul was standing next to the open passenger-side door of Jack's car, not moving. When he saw what his buddy got, the other punk stopped dead in his tracks, holding his hands up in surrender. He backed away slowly as Jack and Raul got back into Jack's car and pulled out of the lot onto Lorena Street. As they

The Journeyman and the Apprentice
drove up to Whittier Boulevard looking for another taco stand, Jack could see in his rear-view mirror the one punk helping the other one with the broken jaw to his feet and into his car.

Jack's adrenaline was pumping. His right hand was beginning to swell and darken. He thought the other guy's jaw must be doing the same thing. He and Raul drove along in silence. It wasn't until they got to the next taco stand that they started talking about it.

"Híjola, ese!" Raul was first to speak. "Yuh tol' me you knew how to box, but, man, I didn't think you were *that* good! When yuh hit that fucking guy, it made the loudest cracking noise I ever heard, eh!"

"Been a long time."

Raul's tone was excited. Jack's was quiet, reflective, subdued, even though his pulse was pounding.

"Remind me never to give *you* bad time, eh."

"Don't know what got into me. Guy j'st pissed me off, man."

"Hey, if him, or somebody in his car, took a shot at you, like you tol' me, you're in the clear."

"Hand's go'n'a be big as a softball by tomorrow. How'm I go'n'a explain it to Carmela, and worse, her mother. She's just startin' to like me. She finds out I just beat the shit out of a chicano, it's all over, man."

"Hey, man, they took a shot at you. You ain't got no problems."

"Yeah, you don't know Teresa."

They finished their burritos and headed back to Cypress Park. Jack drove straight through to Glassell Park and took Raul home. Then he went home and got some ice on his hand.

*   *   *

The next morning at Mass, as he'd thought, it was tough explaining his bruised and swollen hand to Carmela and Teresa. He just came right out and told them exactly what happened starting with the incident after he'd walked Carmela home after they'd visited Gloria. Earlier in the week when Carmela saw the broken window in his car, he didn't tell her the truth about how it got broken. He told her the same thing he'd told the cops. So now he had to come clean on that, too. Teresa took it harder than Carmela, mostly because the punk was a Mexicano, no matter that he'd taken a shot at Jack. He didn't offer to drive the Rángels home,

210

The Journeyman and the Apprentice
rather he bade them goodbye at the church, went straight to his place and spent the day alone nursing his swollen hand.

*   *   *

Jack arrived at Carmela's house at five to eight Monday morning. She was watching for him from the picture window. When he pulled up, she hugged her mother and father goodbye, picked up her new briefcase, and went out the door and down the stairs, meeting him before he got out of the car.

"How's your hand?" she said, leaning over and kissing him on the cheek as he pulled out into the street.

"You c'n see it's still pretty swollen. Your mom still all agüitado at me?"

"I just repeated what you told us. After I explained it again, I think she understood."

They pulled up in front of Gloria's house. She was waiting at the curb. They got on the Arroyo Seco Parkway and headed south. He dropped the girls off on campus at twenty to nine.

"Be back here at two o'clock," he said.

"Okay."

211

They entered a campus that was bustling with first-day-of-school activity. There were lines at the entrance of the bookstore and the admissions office. Throngs of students were hanging around the central quad. Some hurried off to class. Others came in and replaced those who'd left. At ten to nine, Carmela went to class and Gloria got in line at the bookstore. They met at the cafeteria for lunch. It, like every other place on campus, was crowded with students.

"So, how were your classes?" Gloria asked.

"Fun. I like my English teacher. Psychology will be hard. I can't wait to see what biology will be like this afternoon," she said.

"What do you have tomorrow?"

"History and biology lab."

"What time?"

"History's at ten a.m., and biology's at one in the afternoon. You don't have any classes tomorrow, right?"

"That's right. I won't be takeen the streetcar with you on Tuesday and Thursday."

"Jack says he'll drive me every morning and pick me up on Monday afternoons. If you want, you can ride along on your days. We can take the streetcar home on Wednesdays and Fridays."

The Journeyman and the Apprentice

They finished their lunch, went to class, met afterwards, and walked out to Vermont Avenue where Jack was sitting in his car. Raul was with him. The two girls talked about school the whole way home.

"Have you decided where you're going in the fall?" Carmela asked.

"I wouldt love to go to Marymount down Palos Verdes, but it's kind of far away, and I don't think my parents can affordt for me to go there, so I'll probably land up at State. If I go there, I can live at home and take the streetcar and trolley bus. Plus, State's supposed to be a goodt teacher's college. Eventually I want to be a teacher, so it wouldt be perfect for that."

"I can't even think about a place like Marymount. I *know* my parents can't afford it. I'm sure I'll be going to State when I get to upper division."

"Don't talk too soon," Jack said. "Way Carlos and me been cuttin' hair lately, by the time you're ready, he could be makin' enough feria to send yuh to Marymount."

"There's a chance I couldt get a scholarship to Marymount," Gloria said.

"Yuh see," Jack said to Carmela. "Maybe you could get a scholarship, too. You're smart enough."

Jerome Arthur

When Jack dropped Carmela off, Carlos was sitting on his stool in the back of the shop, playing his saxophone. Carmela stuck her head in the door of the shop to greet her father.

"How was your first day?" he asked.

"I had so much fun. My classes will be hard, but they'll be interesting, too."

"That's real swell, honey."

"Thank you for making it possible, Papá."

"You can thank Jack, too. He had a lot to do with it."

Carmela went upstairs and spent the rest of the afternoon in her room doing the homework assignments she'd gotten that day. At five o'clock she closed her books and went into the kitchen to get dinner ready for when her mother got home.

At five-thirty Carlos turned off the lights in the shop and went upstairs. He went straight into the kitchen and got a bottle of Eastside out of the refrigerator. Carmela had something in the oven.

"Mmm, what yuh got cookin'?"

"Tuna casserole."

"Smells good."

He sat down in his easy chair and turned the radio on. Carmela checked the casserole in

214

The Journeyman and the Apprentice

the oven and joined her father in the living room. They sat in silence, listening to Frank Sinatra with the Nelson Riddle band. He sipped his beer, and they watched the rush hour traffic zooming up and down San Fernando Road. The warehouses and manufacturing plants next to the train yard looked ghostly alongside the concrete river channel. It was still light out, so the lights in the neighborhoods along Riverside Drive weren't on yet. It was a pretty view at night. During daylight hours it was just another industrial eyesore with its attendant noise and rampant pollution.

Remembering her casserole, Carmela snapped out of her reverie and went into the kitchen to check on it. Teresa came home as she was setting the table. She put the hot Pyrex dish on a trivet in the center, and they all sat down and dished it up.

"So, how was your first day of school?" Teresa asked.

"I love it," Carmela said. "So much better than work."

"You sound so happy, mijita. I'm glad you finally got what we've all wantedt for so long?"

"You look pretty happy, too."

215

"Because I am happy. It's my last week of night shift."

Teresa's new shift would be from seven a.m. to three p.m. Tuesday through Saturday. For the first time in the five years since she'd been working, she and Carlos would be on the same schedule and have the same two days off. She started having visions of them actually going somewhere on a Monday, like Long Beach. It wouldn't be hard. All they'd have to do is get on the streetcar right out in front, go downtown to the P.E. station, and get enough tokens for a round-trip on the only Red Car left, the Long Beach Limited.

"Everything's changed a lot since Jack came to work for me?" This to Carmela and Teresa, but especially to Teresa.

"*I'll* say," said Carmela. "It's only been three months, and you both seem to be so busy. He just told me again today how busy you are."

"Are you suggesteen I owe him sometheen for getteen my day shift?" Teresa asked Carlos.

"Not at all. I just think he's brought some good luck into our world. That's all."

"All he didt was bring a youthful attitudte and some goodt ideas into your barber shop. He got you motivatedt."

216

The Journeyman and the Apprentice

"Isn't that enough."

"Oh, it's plenty for you, but not necessarily for me."

"I don't understand why you're so hard on Jack," Carmela said. "He's really a nice person, and he's done a lot for all of us. Look at how much mi abuela likes him."

"Listen to me, Carmela. I'm easier on Jack than I am on a lota' gavachos I've known, and some I know right now. You were too young to remember the time we almost got attacked down on Broadtway by those military hoodlums that were goeen around and beateen up Mexicanos. And then the newspapers called the Mexicanos rioters. They called it 'the zoot suit riots.' Blame it on the victims. And your father off fighteen their war! It's a goodt thing he was, too, because if he was home, he might have been with us, and they wouldt have beat him up, too."

"Don't you think it's time to quit beating that horse," Carlos said. "Fact is, I wasn't there, and I didn't get bad treatment in the Navy just because I was a Metsican. Don't get me wrong. I wasn't crazy about military life, but they were mean to everybody, not just Metsicans."

"I'm not so easy to forgive and forget. And look what Jack didt just the other night."

"Oh, mamá! Stop it! You saw what they did to Jack's window. With a gun! He's lucky to be alive. They were not poor, defenseless Mexicans."

Teresa made no response, and there wasn't much more anybody else could say, so they finished dinner, and Carlos went into the living room, Teresa back to work, and Carmela to the kitchen to wash the dishes. When Carmela finished and went back to her room to study, Carlos went down to his shop to work on his second musical composition. At nine-thirty he went back up to the house and got ready to go to the Gateway and walk Teresa home. After he got his winter coat out of the closet, he knocked on Carmela's door to tell her he was going. She said she wanted to go along.

The store was quiet when they entered. Carlos only saw three shoppers. Teresa's was the only open check stand, and at the moment no one was in her line. She kept herself busy by stuffing brown paper bags into the pigeonholes under the counter.

"Not much happening, huh?" Carlos said to her as they approached.

"It's always slow at this late hour."

"Wonder why they stay open so late."

The Journeyman and the Apprentice

"Sometimes we'll get a late rush. Time goes slow when there's no business. It'll go by quicker when I get on my new shift 'cause it's so much busier during the day."

Just then one of the three customers Carlos had seen came up to the check stand with a shopping cart full of groceries. Carlos stood aside as Teresa started checking them. At five to ten, alternating rows of fluorescent ceiling lights went dark, the signal to the last shoppers that the store was closing its doors.

When they got to John's shop on the walk home, Carlos and Carmela stopped to look in the window. Teresa stopped, too, but she stood back as her spouse and daughter cupped their hands around their eyes and got right up to the window and looked in.

"Boy, John ain't got nothin' on me, eh baby?" Carlos said to Carmela.

"This is nice, Papá, but not as nice as yours."

It was the first time he'd looked in John's shop since he'd done all the work on his own. Carmela was right. His shop was a lot nicer than John's. When they got home, Carlos and Carmela looked in *his* window. Teresa looked in through the door. Moments later they climbed the steps to the house and went in.

Jerome Arthur

*   *   *

As Teresa lay next to a sleeping Carlos that night, she couldn't get the conversation she'd had with Carmela earlier out of her head. She kept flashing back to that day in 1943 when she went shopping downtown with her mother and daughter.

...carmela was six years old...just finished first gradte...i don't remember the exact date, but i'll never forget that day in june...mamá wantedt to buy her some summer clothes...got on the streetcar around noon...spent most of the afternoon shoppeen at three stores that day, the broadtway, orbach's, may company...got carmela a wool bathing suit, two sun dresses, leather sandals...came out of the may company and were greetedt by a big commotion...soldiers and sailors runneen up and down the street terrorizeen any mexicanos they saw...señora gonzález saidt her son and his girlfriend were attacked...saidt the soldiers were strippeen the clothes off the men and rapeen the women...when we triedt to get back on the streetcar to go home, those pinchi gringo soldados y marineros were pusheen and shoveen us around...the motorman halped us

The Journeyman and the Apprentice

get on the streetcar...it was surroundedt and barely moved...we saw one mexican teenager surroundedt by a half dozen soldiers who were shouteen obscenities at him....

"...fuckin' greasy spic, get your fuckin' beaner ass the hell outa' here...go back where yuh came from, cholo...."

...one of the soldiers kicked the young man in the groin...i triedt to shield carmela, but couldtn't...she was terrifiedt...the young boy, and that's all he was, looked like a corneredt fox by the hounds in uniform...he hadt terror in his eyes...i hugged carmela to my chest, tryeen to cover her ears and eyes...finally, the streetcar got through the mob, picked up speed, and left the uproar behind...by the time we got home, all three of us were scaredt and shakeen...carmela and me lived in a cottage next door to papá and mamá while carlos was gone to the war...stayedt with mamá that day until papá got home from work...diden't go home until bed-time...huddledt in the liveen room after din-ner...papá was astonished when we toldt him what we saw that day....

"...i don't understand it...how could something like this happen?...he saidt over and over...."

221

Jerome Arthur

...for a while after that, mexicanos all over the city triedt to be more discreet than they were before, and just as quick as the troubles hadt startedt, they endedt...only thing we heardt after, there were a couple small stories in the times...la opiñón *gave a better picture of what really happenedt that day...*the times *article saidt the mexicanos were doeen something subversive, and the service men were doeen their patriotic duty....*

Sixteen

Jack arrived at the shop at eight the next morning. Carmela came down the stairs as he pulled up to the curb. She put her briefcase in the back seat, got in the front and they headed north on Cypress toward Glassell Park. When he got to the intersection of Cypress, Verdugo, Eagle Rock and San Fernando Road, he turned left onto San Fernando and headed north. Carmela gave him a puzzled look. Her curiosity got the best of her after one block on San Fernando.

"Where are we going, Jack?" she asked.

"You have any breakfast before I picked you up?"

"Just a slice of toast and orange juice. Why?"

"That's good. I'm takin' yuh out to breakfast before I take yuh to school."

He pulled into Van de Kamp's parking lot, and they went into the restaurant. Since it was a weekday, it wasn't as busy as it had been

Jerome Arthur

the Sunday they met. They found an empty booth and sat down.

"Aren't you afraid you'll be late for work?" she asked.

"No problem. I squared it with Carlos."

They looked at their menus and ordered when the waitress came with glasses of water and silverware. Jack got a Spanish omelet and a cup of coffee; Carmela ordered a short stack of pancakes and milk. After the waitress left, Jack reached his hands across the table and took Carmela's. His right hand was still swollen and black and blue, even though he'd been packing it in ice the last four nights.

"Couple reasons I brought yuh here. For one thing it's a shorter way to City. Hey, but that's nothin'. Real reason I brought yuh here's 'cause it's the perfect place to tell yuh what I have to say. First time I ever saw yuh was here. So, here goes. I wan'a marry yuh, Carmela? I mean, not right away, but maybe after yuh finish college?"

He took his hands away and reached his left hand into his jacket pocket. He brought out a blue velvet box, popped it open and handed it to her. A half carat diamond sparkled on top of a slender gold band.

"Oh, Jack. It's beautiful."

224

The Journeyman and the Apprentice

"Here, let me put it on yer finger."

He put his hand out, and she gave the box back to him.

"I got it at the same jeweler I got your amethyst. It's the same size, so it should fit."

She'd been wearing the amethyst on her right-hand ring finger. He slipped the diamond onto her left hand. She held both hands out and admired all her new jewelry. She still hadn't formally accepted his proposal, so he sat in silence and looked at her intently.

She finally said, "Yes, I will marry you, but not until I've got my college degree. And you know you're going to have to get my parents' consent. Especially Mamá's."

"That goes without saying. I'll take care of it tonight when we finish cuttin', when your mom comes home for dinner."

"There won't be any problem as long as we make it clear that I'm finishing college. I won't wear the ring until we get their consent. You keep it till then. When you see papá, tell him I've invited you to dinner tonight."

"Okay."

She took the ring off and handed it back to him. He replaced it in the box and put the box back into his jacket pocket. They finished eating and got back on the road to City. He made it to the shop by a quarter to ten and found Joseph Cano sitting in his chair reading the newspaper. Carlos had one in the chair and three waiting.

"You been waitin' long?" Jack asked Joseph.

"About ten minutes. No problem. Carlos told me you was go'n'a be late."

"They were lined up in front when I got here at eight-thirty," Carlos said. "This is my third cut."

Jack no sooner snugged the haircloth around Joseph's neck than the front door opened and another guy came in. The whole day went like that. At twelve-thirty Carlos walked over to the three waiting customers, folding his hair-cloth as he went.

"Hey, guys. I'm going to get some lunch. I'll be back in a half hour."

Jack excused himself from the guy he was working on at that moment and followed Carlos out the door.

"What's up?"

"Carmela told me to tell yuh she invited me up for dinner tonight."

"Good deal."

Carlos went up the steps, and Jack went back into the shop. When Carlos got back, there were still three waiting. The one in his chair

226

The Journeyman and the Apprentice

made it four. Jack took his lunch break after he'd finished the cut he was working on. Forty-five minutes later when he came back, there were still three waiting, and there were three waiting for the rest of the day until five-thirty. That was when Carlos locked the door and turned the sign around. He wanted to make sure he and Jack got out of there in time to sit down with Teresa when she got there. It took her fifteen minutes to walk home and back to the store, and that only left her half an hour to have dinner. Carmela had come home from school at three-thirty.

Jack finished before Carlos. They were both done when Teresa approached.

"Let's leave everything like it is and go upstairs right now," Carlos said. "We can come down and clean up after Teresa goes back to work. I'm coming back down here then anyway."

"Let's go."

As they came out of the shop, Teresa was just starting up the steps, and they fell in behind her. The aroma of freshly cooked chicken enchiladas trailed Carmela as she came out of the kitchen. After Teresa hung up her coat, she went into the bathroom and washed up. When she came out, they all sat down at the dinner table. Carmela had set the table with their best china and silverware.

"So, why the fancy place setteens?" Teresa asked as they began eating. "And why are you all dressed up? Not that I mind. You look very beautiful tonight, mijita."

"Jack and I have an announcement."

The smile went away from Teresa's face as Jack brought out the velvet box, but before she could say anything, he said,

"I asked Carmela to marry me this morning, and she accepted my proposal, but she said I needed your consent, so she invited me here tonight so I could ask you for it."

"That's fantastic!" Carlos said. "You got my permission!"

"I only have one question," Teresa said with a grave look on her face. "When? 'Cause the only way I'll say yes will be if you tal me you don't plan on getteen marriedt till after Carmela finishes college."

"Oh, absolutely," Jack said. "In fact, that's the first thing I said to Carmela after I asked her. We're go'n'a have a long engagement."

"That's all I care about. You have my permission, too."

The Journeyman and the Apprentice

But she wasn't as enthusiastic as Carlos, and that caused Carmela slight concern.

After dinner when Teresa had gone and Carmela started doing the dishes, Carlos and Jack went downstairs to count the money and clean up the shop. They'd grossed a hundred and ten dollars between them fifty for Jack and sixty for Carlos. Jack's tips added up to seven dollars. When they'd cleaned up the shop and secured it, Jack went back up the stairs to the house. He asked Carmela if she wanted to go for a drive up to Griffith Park. Carlos stayed in the shop and worked on his music.

*   *   *

As they sat in the car watching the shimmering city lights, she was snuggled up close to him and he kissed her. He was taken by an impulse, and he moved his left hand from where he was holding her around the waist up her right flank to her breast. Her first reaction to this was to move into it, or so it seemed to Jack, but it was a fleeting response, for in the next instant her hand moved to his wrist and she gently but firmly moved his hand away. Then she pulled away from him, but she wasn't exactly sure why. She had very mixed feelings about what was going on. There was no doubt she liked the firm feel of Jack's hand on her breast (his touch prompted a rare and delicious tingling in her nipple), but then something else told her, she wasn't sure what, that she wasn't supposed to be doing this.

"Uh, oh. I guess that was the wrong thing to do, huh?" he said looking downcast and dispirited.

"Gosh, I don't know, Jack. It sure feels good when we're like that, but somehow it just doesn't seem right. I'm sure Mamá wouldn't approve. It's getting late. If you're going to pick Gloria and me up at eight tomorrow morning, we both should be getting home soon."

He knew she was right. They really should be getting back to the house. There was just nothing else for it at that point. So, with a sigh of despair, he pushed the starter button on the dashboard, and the car settled into a smooth idle. He shifted into reverse, backed out and coasted down the hill and back into the reality of the city. They were silent the whole drive back to Cypress Avenue. Jack was thinking he'd blown it pretty badly with Carmela, even to the point that she might want to break off the engagement. When he pulled up to the curb in front of the shop, he was expecting her to jump

230

The Journeyman and the Apprentice

out of the car and run from him as quickly as she could get away, but he was surprised when she kept her seat after he shut the motor off.

"Listen, Carmela, I'm sorry if I got outa' line tonight, but I couldn't help it. I love you so much."

"Oh, Jack, honey. It wasn't that bad. It's like I told you. There was something about it that I liked too, but I think we should slow down. We've only known each other for three months, and we're already engaged. You're the first boy I've ever gotten this close to, and I like it. I just think we should slow down."

She twisted into him and at the same time put her right hand on the back of his neck and pulled him toward her. She reached up with her left hand and pushed his hat off. He offered no resistance, and they fell together. When they parted, she reached for the door handle and nudged the door ajar.

"I've got to get upstairs and you've got to get home. It's late. I'll see you tomorrow morning. I love you."

"Likewise," he said. "I'll talk to you tomorrow."

He waited in his car until she disappeared up the steps, and then he made a U-turn from the curb and drove home.

231

Seventeen

By mid March the shop was so busy that Carlos couldn't find time anymore to get across the street to read the Eight Star with Enrique. Just as well. Carlos' good fortune seemed to be rubbing off on Enrique as his store was getting just as busy as Carlos' shop. The only day they could get together for sure was Sunday when both of their shops were closed. Carlos had Monday off, and he would go across the street and visit, but that was Enrique's first day back to work after his day off, and it was usually a busy day.

"Funny, eh, how my business is pickeen up, too," Enrique said one busy Monday between customers as Carlos read the paper.

The gray and overcast morning had only hinted at the rain that was now coming down in a steady shower.

"Well, that's good, ain't it?"

The Journeyman and the Apprentice

"Oh, I ain't complaineen. It's just kind of funny how it's rubbed off is all."

"I'm so busy I can't even get over here no more."

"That ain't no lie, eh. I barely ever see you no more."

When Carlos finished skimming through the paper, he stuck around for a few more minutes and talked to Contreras as he rang up sales on his cash register.

...hell, i ain't got nothing else to do...maybe go over to the house and see if teresa'd like to go to a late afternoon matinee...schedule in the paper says east of eden *is playing at the orpheum....*

Contreras started a long run of customers, and Carlos really couldn't talk to him, so he left. Teresa was sitting in her place on the couch working her knitting needles.

"Wha'da yuh say we go to a movie?" he said. "Great matinee weather."

"Sounds like fun, but don't you think we shouldt wait for Carmela to come home from school."

"What for? We can leave her a note. She could fix her own dinner, and we could get something to eat downtown after the show."

"I don't know; I guess we couldt go but isn't it goeen to be expensive."

Teresa was still not used to their recent prosperity, and she had her doubts whether it would last.

"Just can't get over how poor you been, huh? Don't worry about the feria. We got it. Now, go get ready, and don't forget your rain-coat and umbrella."

They left a note on the dining room table and started toward the door. When Carlos opened it for Teresa, Carmela was standing on the other side holding her key to the lock. They told her quickly what they were doing, and then rushed down the stairs to catch the streetcar that was rolling up to the safety zone as they approached.

Carmela went into her room and took her coat off. Then she went into the kitchen and turned the gas on under the tea kettle. She got a cup out of the cupboard, put a tea bag in and set it on the counter next to the heating water. She went back to her room to get her English and psych. texts, and a notebook and pen. She brought everything out and set it all down on the dining room table. That's when she saw the note. The tea kettle started whistling, so she turned off the gas and poured the boiling water

The Journeyman and the Apprentice

over the tea bag. She took the cup over to the table, set it down, opened her English book and started reading the assignment she'd gotten that day in class.

*   *   *

After Jack had dropped Carmela off, he went to his place to get in out of the rain. He opened a bottle of beer and sat down to read *The American*. He read for about an hour before dozing off with the book in his lap. When he awoke, he decided to go downtown and get some dinner at Clifton's. He found a parking place right on Broadway across the street from the restaurant. As he stepped to the curb and waited for the signal to change, he saw Carlos and Teresa heading toward the restaurant. When the signal changed and he crossed the street, they had already entered. He trotted over and got inside just as they were entering the tunnel that led to the steam tables.

"Carlos, Teresa!" he said. He always used the Spanish pronunciation.

They both turned and Carlos said, "Hey, what're you doing here?"

"Gettin' somethin' to eat. Looks like that's what you guys're doin', too?"

"Yeah, we are. Just saw *East of Eden* down the street, and now we're go'n'a go have some dinner before we go home. Wan'a join us?"

"Thanks. That'd be great. Yuh wan'a ride home, after?"

"Sure."

They got their food and found a table on the front mezzanine by the window overlooking the hustle and bustle of Seventh and Broadway. Carlos' customer, Peter, was working that section at the time, and he came over and visited with them for a few minutes.

"Look, the rain's gettin' heavier," Jack said after Peter went back to work. "Good thing we ran into each other. You'd get soaked if you had to go out there and wait for a streetcar. My car may look like a heap, but it's warm and dry inside, and it'll get yuh home every time."

As it was, they got wet just getting to the car. They were greeted by a steady downpour when they left the restaurant. Teresa popped open her umbrella, and staying close together, they crossed the street to the car. Jack drove; Carlos rode shotgun; Teresa rode in the back seat. The rain got lighter as they drove up North Broadway, and when they pulled up to the curb

The Journeyman and the Apprentice

in front of the shop, it had turned to a light shower.

"Wan'a beer?" Carlos asked Jack. "You could talk to Carmela, too. She's prob'ly studying, but I know she'd take a break if you came up."

"Sounds good."

They hurried up the stairs. It was almost eight o'clock. Carmela greeted them at the front door and welcomed them into the warm and toasty house. Jack stood by the window and looked through the mist at the twinkling neighborhood lights while the women prepared the drinks and Carlos tuned the radio to his favorite jazz station.

When they were settled—the men with their bottles of Eastside, the women with cups of hot chocolate—Teresa picked up her knitting needles. Jack stuck around and chatted with the family for another half hour. Carmela walked him to the door and stepped out onto the front porch with him. They hugged and kissed and Jack said,

"So, see yuh tomorrow morning, right?"

"Eight o'clock. I love you."

"Love you, too."

He kissed her one more time and headed down the steps. The rain had let up and the tem-

237

perature had dropped. The streets were glassy and water was standing in the gutters. He got home at a little before nine.

*   *   *

The next morning Jack dropped Carmela off at school and got back to the shop by a quarter to nine. By now he and Carlos had reached the point that two or three customers would be waiting at the front door of the shop several days a week at that hour, for sure on Tuesdays, Fridays and Saturdays, consistently the busiest days of the week. Although Wednesdays and Thursdays were slow by comparison, they were still busier now than the busiest days before Jack arrived on the scene. The two barbers had got so busy that Carlos was thinking about raising the price of a haircut from three dollars to three-fifty. They both only had a few regulars who wanted to make appointments.

Carlos came down the steps, and when he got to the bottom, Jack approached from the crosswalk. There were two customers waiting at the shop's front door. They sat down in the two chairs as the barbers turned on the lights and heat.

238

The Journeyman and the Apprentice

Shortly after lunch the phone rang and Carlos picked it up.

"Hello, Carlos?" the voice on the other end of the line said.

"Yeah?"

"Think I c'n get your last appointment today for a haircut?"

"Absolutely." Carlos' self-confidence was growing by the day. "Here, let me write yuh down in my appointment book. What's yer name?"

"Gerry Mulligan. Want my phone number, too? Case yuh need to reach me?"

Carlos was momentarily dumb struck. If this was the Gerry Mulligan he was thinking of, he was Carlos' favorite sax player.

"Want it or not?" Mulligan said.

"Oh…yeah…yeah."

Carlos wrote down the number Mulligan gave him and told him he'd see him at five-thirty. He was filled with anticipation the rest of the day. Gerry Mulligan showed up at five-twenty-five, and he was indeed the great baritone saxophonist.

"Who told yuh to call me?" Carlos said as he towel dried Gerry's red hair, prepping it to give him his trademark crew cut/flat top.

239

"One of your customers is a good friend of a buddy of mine. I don't know what his name is. My buddy says you play the saxophone. That right? I see you got an instrument over there."

"Hey, I'm just learning."

"Yeah? Me too. Yuh know, my axe is out in the car. How about I go out and get it after you're done with the haircut? We could jam for a while. You into that?"

Now Carlos was really speechless. He mustered his confidence and said,

"Yeah, sure."

Carlos had locked the door and turned the sign around when Gerry sat in his chair, so by the time he finished with him, Jack had finished his last cut. As Carlos cleaned up his workstation and swept the floor, Gerry went out to his car to get his instrument. When Jack left, he told Carlos he'd go upstairs and tell the women he'd be late getting home. Then Carlos and Gerry—he couldn't believe it—jammed till about seven-thirty.

And that was the beginning of a five-year relationship. Gerry became a standing appointment in Carlos' book every other Tuesday at five-thirty, except when he was on the road. He'd bring his sax every time, and he and Carlos would jam for about an hour and a half after

The Journeyman and the Apprentice

the haircut. Gerry even played a couple of the tunes Carlos had composed at one of his live gigs. Carlos actually went on to compose a number of tunes in the years ahead, but none of them were ever recorded by anybody. He didn't really care about that anyway. He was doing it for his own enjoyment.

Eighteen

Mid morning the Monday before Easter, Señora Guevara went to visit her daughter to discuss the family's plans for the upcoming holiday. Teresa was alone in the house. Jack had taken Carlos to Long Beach to visit Carlos' cousin, Julian. Carmela was on spring break from school, so on their way to Long Beach, Jack and Carlos dropped her and Gloria off at the public library on Hope Street. Señora Guevara was huffing and puffing by the time she got to the top of the stairs.

"Entre, mamá. ¿Como estás?"

"¡Whew! Out of breath. Those steps will surely matame in the end."

"Would you like una taza de café?" Teresa asked as she went into the kitchen.

The Journeyman and the Apprentice

"Sí, mijita," said Señora Guevara as she sat down at the dining room table. "¿Are you finally settled en su trabajo nuevo?"

Teresa came out of the kitchen carrying a small round tray laden with two cups of coffee and a plate of pan dulce.

"Pues, sí. I like my new hours, and I got a pay raise, también."

"Bueno. I am happy that your trabajo es mejor. ¿But what about Carmela? ¿Shouldn't you and she be planning a wedding? She's engaged to Jack. ¿Porqué esperan?"

"She needs to get her education first. Only then, should she think of marriage or whatever else she wants to do. No me importa as long as she finishes school."

"Quizás you are right."

They planned out Easter Sunday from nine o'clock mass to the dinner they'd serve. It would not be as elaborate as Thanksgiving or Christmas. It would be a simple Mexican dinner: chicken enchiladas, beans and rice, and they wouldn't have all the company they had on those holidays. The family only, plus Jack, whom they all now considered a family member. By the time they'd arranged everything, their coffee cups were empty. They cleared the dining room table, took the cups into the kitchen and washed them. As they finished cleaning up, Teresa suggested that they go window shopping along Cypress Avenue on their walk to Señora Guevara's house.

As they were passing the appliance store, they stopped to look at the televisions on display in the window. They looked at the flickering screens and checked the prices. The fifteen-inch Emerson console she'd seen last week was still there, and now it had a yellow tag with red letters that said "REDUCED." They had lowered the price from two hundred to one-hundred-seventy-five dollars. Another tag read, "Easy Terms." The two ladies stood on the sidewalk and watched "Search for Tomorrow" flicker silently on the screen. In that moment Teresa decided that it was about time that the Rángels had a television set.

"Vamos a entrar, mamá. I'm going to buy that televisión."

"¿Can you afford it, mijita?"

"Sí. I got a pay raise. ¿Remember? Carlitos is making más dinero ahora, también."

And so they went inside the store, and Teresa bought a television set. She gave them fifty dollars cash and signed a contract to pay the rest in twelve monthly installments of twelve dollars each. Rabbit ears and a rooftop

The Journeyman and the Apprentice

antenna were both included. The appliance store delivered all of it to the Rángel household at one-thirty. Teresa got back from her mother's and was home when it arrived. After the service person put the box with the antenna in it on the back patio, he installed the rabbit ears and plugged the T.V. in. Carmela got home from the library as the man who'd installed it was pulling away from the curb. She was just in time to see the opening credits for *Edge of Night.*

"Mamá, you bought a television!"

"About time we got one."

Carmela put her books in her room and joined her mother on the couch. They watched that show and just started a *Superman* rerun when Carlos and Jack came in at three o'clock.

"Bonaroo!" Carlos said when he saw the T.V. "Funny, I was thinking about taking you two out next Monday to look at televisions. You beat me to it."

"How cool!" Jack said. He was looking at the wood finish on the console.

"We get twelve channels," Teresa said. "The man that installedt it, toldt me that the ones that aren't real clear, will clear up when you put the antenna up on the roof."

She walked over to the set and went through the channels with the selector knob.

245

Channel one was the only one with no programming.

"That's real keen!" said Jack.

"Wouldt you like to come to dinner tonight and watch the television after?" Teresa asked him.

"Yeah, sure. That'd be great. What time? Six?"

"That wouldt be fine."

"Did you and Papá have a good time at uncle Julian's?" Carmela asked.

"Yeah, we went to this real cool beer joint called Joe Jost for lunch. They give yuh a beer in a sixteen-ounce glass that looks like a great big chalice. They call 'em schooners, and they only cost two bits. We ate pickled eggs and Joe's Specials—Polish sausage and Swiss on rye with mustard and a pickle. Must have five pool tables there. Shot a couple games. You get a lot done down the library?"

"Yes. I worked a lot on my English research paper. I'm going back tomorrow to finish the research. After that all I have to do is write it, and I could finish that before I go back to class on Monday."

"That's great!"

He was responding to her excitement. He didn't really know the details of what she

246

The Journeyman and the Apprentice

was talking about and didn't really care about it for its own sake. He was just glad because she was glad.

Jack went home at four o'clock and got ready for his dinner date with the Rángels. Carmela and her mother started getting dinner ready at five-thirty. Jack arrived at six. After dinner he and Carmela did the dishes as Carlos and Teresa got settled in the living room. After watching the television for a couple of hours, Jack said his goodbyes and left.

It had been a couple weeks since he'd seen Raul, so he decided to take a drive up to his house before going home. Jack hung out with him till ten o'clock. As he drove down Cypress on his way home, he looked in the shop, which was lighted, and saw Carlos working with his sax. In the picture window he saw Teresa's silhouette. She was knitting in her usual place on the couch. He continued on his way, and when he got home, he listened to the radio for a short time, and then he was in bed and asleep.

At midnight Teresa got out of bed to go to the bathroom, and she heard the radio playing softly in the other room. When she came out, she went into the living room and found Carlos sound asleep in his easy chair. As she turned off the radio light, he came to and stood up. They went into the bedroom, and she got back into bed as he changed into his pajamas.

*   *   *

Easter week in the shop was busy. Customers were lined up at the front door every morning, and there were always three waiting throughout each one of those days. On Good Friday Carlos took off between noon and three to go to church with Teresa and Señora Guevara for the stations of the cross. Jack kept the shop open except between one and two to go to lunch. Saturday was as busy as any other day-before-the-holiday. The two barbers sat in the shop that evening drinking ice-cold Eastsides and musing on how busy the week had been. Jack made almost two hundred dollars, and Carlos a hundred and seventy-six.

After Mass on Sunday, Jack drove the family to Carlos' house. The three ladies made chorizo con huevos for breakfast. Everybody but Jack had received communion, but he had fasted anyway, so they were all hungry by the time breakfast was served. When they'd finished eating, Carlos and Jack went up on the roof and installed the T.V. antenna. It took them a couple of hours to complete the job. When it

248

The Journeyman and the Apprentice

was up, the picture was much sharper on all twelve channels. Carmela told Jack she wanted to go for a drive, so they left the others watching the Judy Garland/Fred Astaire movie *Easter Parade* on television.

"So, where yuh wan'a go?" Jack asked as they walked down the stairs.

"I've never seen that school you went to. Show it to me."

"Okay."

Since he thought of that time in his life as an embarrassment, he was hesitant to show any part of it to anybody. For his part, he'd like to forget it, but then again, he did have some pleasant memories of the place. It *was* high school, after all. She'd been curious about the place ever since he'd first told her about it. So now here she was, and she realized there wasn't much to see. It consisted of two buildings set back on the property at the end of a gated drive. The campus was deserted.

"It's quiet 'cause it's Easter. Holidays yuh git to go home. Any other Sunday'd be visitor's day, and there'd be a lota' cars parked in that drive. Building on the left is the classrooms. One on the right is the dorm. Me and my buddies used to sneak out on weekends…go over to

249

Eagle Rock...play miniature golf at the course on Colorado Boulevard."

"You were allowed to go off campus?" she asked.

"Weekends only. And we weren't really allowed. It was just easier to sneak out on the days yuh didn't have class. If yuh played on the baseball team, you could leave with the team to go play games. I was boxing, so I got outa' there a lot to go work out with the P.A.L."

"How was the school part of it?"

"Prob'ly not much different'n where you went. I bet the discipline was stricter than what you had. I know, I know. That's supposed to be the main thing with Catholic schools, but we were a bunch a' juvies, and we needed it more'n you guys. I only remember one teacher that couldn't control the class. Geometry. Only thing I remember liking in any a' my classes was some Jack London stories we had to read."

He turned the key on, pushed the starter button and moved out into traffic.

"Where to now?" he asked.

"Let's go to your place," she replied.

His heart jumped at this response. When he turned to look at her, she simply smiled and nodded. The first cross street he came to, he turned in and got the car turned around so that

250

The Journeyman and the Apprentice

he could head south on Figueroa. Neither of them spoke on the trip. When he pulled up to the curb in front of his house, he went around to her side and opened the door for her. She looked at him and then batted her eyes away as she stepped out of the car. They walked back to his cottage holding hands. Once inside the house, Jack moved around picking the things up he'd left lying around that morning.

"Could I fix yuh a cupa' coffee, or, here, I think I got some soda in the ice box," he said opening the refrigerator door. He took out a quart bottle of Seven Up.

"Okay," she said, and he poured two glasses, handed her one and sat down next to her on the couch.

They drank their sodas in silence for a few minutes and then put them down on the coffee table in front of them. It was then that Jack slid over so that he was right next to her, and he put his arm around her and kissed her hard and deep. She fell into it, and before either of them knew how it happened, they were on the bed entwined in each others arms.

As they lay there afterward, Carmela had mixed feelings of guilt and joy. Jack was feeling pure joy. He lay propped up on a pillow, fingers laced behind his head, a self-satisfied grin on his face. Carmela lay on her side facing him, her knitted brow betraying the worry in her heart. She wasn't worried about getting pregnant because she'd prepared for that possibility. She'd gone out with Gloria a week earlier and bought a diaphragm. She was mostly letting her Catholic guilt get the best of her.

...good girls don't go to bed with boys before they get married, especially not on easter sunday....

"Do you love me?" she asked.

"Of course I love you, and I always will," he replied taking her in his arms. "We're engaged. We're go'n'a get married."

"I know. But it seems so far off."

They cleaned up, got dressed and went out to Jack's car. The afternoon was moving to evening, and as they traveled down Figueroa, Carmela watched the sun drop in the sky off to the right. Melancholy was setting in. There was still plenty of daylight left as they pulled up in front of the barber shop. Teresa gave them a skeptical look as they entered. Carmela didn't look her straight in the eye. The two young people sat down with Carlos and Teresa and watched the little screen. The show was "The Twentieth Century" with Walter Cronkite, and it had something to do with the German concen-

The Journeyman and the Apprentice

tration camps during the war. Jack stayed until the end of the show, and then he went home.

Nineteen

Jack was euphoric on his drive over to pick up Carmela the next morning. He was in love. He lay awake late Sunday night thinking about her, still smelling her fragrance on his pillow, wondering if she was feeling what he was feeling. Approaching the intersection of Figueroa and Marmion Way, he got mired in traffic which had slowed almost to a standstill.

Up ahead a policeman was waving cars through the intersection against the red light. A Chevy was straddling the broken white line between the two southbound lanes. Sticking out of its side was a panel truck with a ladder rammed violently through the shattered windshield on the passenger side and resting on the hood just inches from the Chevy.

There was a patrol car parked behind the wreckage, and the gumball machine on its roof was turning frantically, spraying the overcast morning with flecks of red and blue. Jack pro-

The Journeyman and the Apprentice

ceeded cautiously through the intersection following the patrolman's directions. Another policeman was talking to a woman, probably the driver of the Chevy, and a man in white overalls and a white painter's cap. He drove through the intersection and stepped on the gas.

As he approached the house, he saw Carmela standing on the sidewalk in front of the shop, her briefcase on the sidewalk at her feet. He pulled up and said through the open passenger side window,

"Hey, schoolgirl. Wan'a lift? I just happen to be goin' that way."

"You nut."

"Better watch what yuh say. I'm your chauffeur."

Gloria was also standing on the sidewalk when they pulled up to her house. Carmela scooted over and snuggled up to Jack. She tilted her head up and kissed him on the cheek. He turned and looked at her, thrilled by her affection. She stayed close to him all the way to school. He put his arm around her shoulder, and she shifted the gears. Gloria rode in silence next to them.

They arrived at the college at twenty-five after eight. Since it was Monday morning, Jack didn't have to hurry to get to the barber shop, so he went to the cafeteria with the girls and had coffee with them before they went off to their classes. Gloria went to the library, leaving Jack alone with Carmela in the cafeteria. Delighted just to be with her and making no attempt to conceal it, Jack watched her, hardly hearing anything she said, as she told him all the things she was going to do that day. At five to nine, they tossed their paper coffee cups and started to walk to her class. The teacher was putting his lecture notes on the lectern. Carmela gave Jack a cursory kiss and started for the door, but he caught her by the forearm and gently pulled her back, giving her a better kiss and a good strong hug. He heard the teacher calling roll above the students' subdued murmur when she opened the classroom door and disappeared inside. He headed back to his car. He drove down Cypress Avenue on his way home.

*   *   *

No sooner did Jack pass the shop than Carlos stepped out the front door of the house and started down the stairs. He crossed the street to Enrique Contreras' grocery store. He and Teresa had eaten breakfast with Carmela. After she left for school, they watched a bit of *The Today*

The Journeyman and the Apprentice

Show, and then Carlos went into the bathroom to take his shower. After that he headed out the door to go visit Enrique. When he left Enrique, he went over to the shop to work on his music. He played for a couple of hours and went back up to the house.

"Any good movies you'd maybe like to go see?" he asked Teresa.

"Do you want to go to a movie?"

"Only if there's something good playing, and you wan'a go, too."

"There's a Cantínflas movie playeen at the Million Dollar."

"Yeah, that sounds good. He's a good comedian. What time?"

"Let's look," she said as she retrieved the morning paper and found the entertainment section. "The first matinee begins at two."

"What time you wan'a leave?"

"Whenever you want."

"We could go early, grab a bite before the movie starts? Shrimp house down Second and Main, couple blocks away."

"Okay, but I got'a get ready."

"Go 'head on. I'm ready when you are."

Teresa was ready by eleven-thirty, and they went down to catch the next streetcar into downtown. It had been overcast all morning.

Now storm clouds were gathering, and it was dark, looking like rain. On their walk from the shrimp house to the movie theater, it started to sprinkle. They came out of the show into a steady downpour. They hadn't dressed for the rain, and they hadn't brought an umbrella, so they waited for the streetcar under the awning of a "jewelry/loan" store near the corner of Third and Broadway. They dashed to the safety zone when the Five Eagle Rock pulled up. The hardwood benches in the streetcar were cold comfort for the rainy, dreary trip home. When they crossed the Broadway bridge, they looked at the water spilling out of the center trough of the concrete riverbed. They looked at each other and held hands.

"Sure is nice to be in a dry place on a day like this," Carlos said.

"Sí, mijito."

The downpour had turned to drizzle when they got off the streetcar in front of the shop. They didn't have to run as they'd done when they boarded. The house was warm, and the light was on in the dining room. Carmela's books and notebooks were open and spread out on the table, but she was nowhere to be seen. As Carlos and Teresa stood by the table, she sud-

258

denly appeared out of the hallway that led to the bedrooms and bathroom.

"Hi," she said. She had a sheepish look on her face. "Where have you guys been?"

"We went to lunch and a movie," Teresa said. "It's warm in here. You must've gotten home from school early."

"I think I got here right after you guys left."

The bathroom door clicked open, and Jack walked up the hall toward them.

"Hi," he said, averting his eyes to one side. "I been hangin' with Carmela all after-noon."

"So we can *see*," Teresa said. Darkness fell across her brow as she spoke. She wanted to ask him what else he'd done, but she was afraid lest he give her an honest answer.

Seeing her mother's black look, and de-tecting the sarcasm in her voice, Carmela said, "I don't know what you're thinking, Mamá, but things aren't how they look here. Jack stayed with me after he brought me home. He's been reading and I've been studying. He just now went to the bathroom, and while he was in there, I went to my room to get another pen because the other one ran out of ink."

259

She held up a Scripto ballpoint pen for Teresa to see. Carlos backed away; he didn't want to discuss this now.

"Well," said Jack, walking over to the dining room table and picking up his book, "I guess I should go home. See yuh at eight in the morning?" This to Carmela, and to Carlos, "I'll see you after I drop her off. Buenas tardes, Señora Rángel."

He left the house, hardly making a sound when he exited. After he was gone, the three family members stood milling around in silence for a few minutes, and then Carmela went back to her books as her parents went over to the coat rack by the front door and took off their wet jackets. Teresa went to the kitchen and started fixing something for dinner, and Carlos sat in his chair next to the radio looking out the window at the rainy day. In deference to Carmela's studying, he didn't turn the radio on, but at length she cleared her things off the table and took them to her room. When she came back out to the kitchen to help Teresa get dinner ready, Carlos turned on the T.V. and watched the news.

"You know how we've told you to never have a boy with you in the house when you're alone," Teresa said a half hour later at the dinner

260

The Journeyman and the Apprentice

table. "I thought you knew better than to do such a thing. What do people think when they see you come in with Jack, and he still hasn't left two hours later?"

"We didn't do anything wrong."

Carmela felt a twinge of guilt when she said this. She thought about the day before at Jack's house.

"Yes, but the people who saw you come in don't know that. You'll land up with a badt reputation."

"It's just not a good thing to do, honey," Carlos finally said to his daughter.

Those nine words, spoken so softly, seemed to put an end to the discussion.

"You're right. It's your house, and I should be more considerate of your feelings. If he comes up to the house with me again, and you guys aren't home, we'll just sit out in front where we can be seen. And if it's raining like today, I'll send him home."

"That wouldt be fine," Teresa said.

*   *   *

When Jack picked Carmela up the next morning, his first question was,

261

"What'd your mom and dad say after I left yesterday?"

"Oh, nothing really. They've always told me never to invite a boy into the house when they're not there. I really *do* know better, and we shouldn't have been in there by ourselves. I apologized and told them I wouldn't do it again."

"Is your mom all agüitado at me?"

"I wouldn't say she's angry at you; I'd just say she still doesn't trust you completely; she's still suspicious of your intentions."

"And she's right, you know; my intentions aren't always entirely honorable."

She picked up on the irony he was expressing. He dropped her off at class and drove straight back to the shop.

Twenty

It had stopped raining early Monday evening, but it started up again sometime after midnight and continued through most of the night. Tuesday morning before daybreak, the clouds had cleared out, and as the sun rose, the day turned bright and crystal-clear. Steam arose from the roof ridges and fence tops, and water trickled down the gutters. The rain had cleansed the air, leaving a glow on the city's morning blush. The storm was followed by a prevailing breeze that kept the skies clear throughout the day.

Carlos was sitting at the dining room table reading the morning *Times*. He'd gotten a subscription when both he and Contreras got so busy that he couldn't get over to the store afternoons to read the *Herald Express* Eight Star.

"Good morning, Papá." Carmela said as she joined him.

"Hi, honey."

She went to the kitchen and started fixing breakfast.

"Did Mamá get over the tizzy fit she was having yesterday?" she asked as she set two dishes on the table.

"She ain't talkin' about it, but yuh know she ain't go'n'a get over it any time soon. That's just how she is."

"She seems to thrive on anxiety and worry."

"Been that way her whole life. Ain't go'n'a change now."

Just then Teresa came out of the hall that led to the bedrooms and bathroom. Her hair was still wet from the shower.

"Were you talkeen about me?" she asked using a towel on her hair.

"Not really," Carlos said.

Carmela had left the breakfast fixings on the kitchen counter next to the stove, so Teresa made herself something to eat. She sat down with her food just as Carlos and Carmela were finishing. They sat and chatted for a while, and then Carmela got up to go to the bathroom to take her shower and get ready for school. Teresa finished eating as Carmela was getting out of the shower. She went into the bathroom and

The Journeyman and the Apprentice

brushed her teeth and was on her way to work by a quarter to seven.

After Jack picked up Carmela, Carlos took his shower and went down to the shop at five to nine. Three customers were lined up at the door when he got there. By now he'd quit going down a half hour ahead of time because if he did, he'd just have to start a half hour early.

Jack showed up a few minutes later, and the two barbers began another busy first day of the week. They got their first break at ten-thirty. That is, Carlos got a break; Jack was working on a customer, and he had one waiting. As he swept the floor, Carlos looked across the street and saw Señora Guevara enter Contreras' grocery store. By the time he finished sweeping, she was walking down the street toward her house. He crossed the street and went into the little market.

"¿Qué pasa, carnal?" Enrique said as Carlos entered. "Lookeen busy over there, eh."

"How it is anymore, 'specially Tuesday, 'cause it's the first daya' the week."

No sooner did Carlos say this than a customer went into the barber shop, so he left the store and went back across the street. By now, the pavement was dry, but there were still puddles of water standing in the low spots of the gutters. The customer Jack had been working on passed Carlos in the doorway as he entered the shop. The one who'd been waiting got into Jack's chair, and the one who'd just entered got into Carlos' chair. The two barbers then stayed busy through the rest of the day, both having to excuse themselves to the waiting customers to get away to lunch.

Carmela was home from school by three o'clock, followed shortly by her mother. She spent the rest of the afternoon studying at the dining room table. At five-thirty she cleared the table and took all of her things to her room. She returned to the kitchen and started helping Teresa put together a casserole for the evening meal. They got it into the oven by six o'clock. Then Teresa tuned the T.V. to Douglas Edwards doing the "C.B.S. Evening News." Moving over to the couch, Teresa sat down with her knitting, and Carmela looked out the living room window and saw Jack emerging from the shop and crossing the street to Contreras' market. She watched him come out of the store carrying a brown paper sack, and head back to the shop. When he reached the middle of the street, he looked up and saw her in the window. She waved to him and he waved back. Then she sat down on the

The Journeyman and the Apprentice
couch and joined her mother watching the conclusion of the fifteen-minute newscast.

When Carlos and Jack finished their beers, they closed the shop and went up the steps to the house. Teresa might still be angry at Jack and Carmela for their behavior yesterday, but that didn't stop her from inviting him to dinner. It seemed she had finally relented and was now more accepting of him as part of the family.

The women turned the television off when the men entered. Teresa took the casserole out of the oven, and they all gathered around the table. She led them in saying grace, and then the women told the men all the things they'd done that day as they ate dinner. After the women finished doing the dishes, Carmela went to her room and brought out the essay she'd been working on earlier and asked Carlos to look it over. It was a paper for her English 1B class. The teacher had asked the class to narrow down the general topic of "The Music of Poetry," and write an essay using the expository method of comparison and contrast. Carmela's essay was a comparison/contrast of the piano styles of Nat "King" Cole (jazz) and Fats Domino (rock 'n' roll) and how each style related to the lyrics of the songs they sang.

"What do I know about it, honey?" Carlos asked.

"Just read it. I think you'll find you actually know a lot about it. It's about Nat "King" Cole and Fats Domino."

"Oh, okay."

She watched the expression on his face as he read. His lips moved as his eyes went back and forth across the page. From time to time he'd whisper a phrase and follow it with a smile.

"Pretty good," he said when he finished. "You really think this guy Fats Domino is that good?"

"Different than Cole, but just as good."

"Could you play me a Fats Domino record? I wan'a hear what it sounds like."

"Sure. Got one on my record player right now."

Jack went with them to Carmela's room as Teresa stayed in the living room knitting and watching T.V.

"Yeah, I heard this before," Carlos said as they listened to "Blue Monday." "Sounds good. I like the sax."

"More primitive than Cole, but just as good."

"Bet you get an A on that paper."

"I hope so."

The Journeyman and the Apprentice

They joined Teresa back in the living room. "I Love Lucy" was just coming on. They watched it and *Cheyenne,* and then Jack got up to leave. Carmela saw him to the front porch. Closing the door behind her, she gave him a strong kiss and hug.

"I love you," he told her as they hugged.

"And I love you."

When she re-entered the house, her mother was just switching off the television. Carlos stood by the living room window and stared out at the dark mountain across the valley. Carmela said good night to her parents and started down the hall to her room. Teresa put her knitting things aside and followed her. Carlos stayed by the window looking out at the winking stars in the black sky. His eyes came back down to the mountain, the river and train yard, finally resting on the deserted street directly below him. He watched a streetcar slide slowly by. Moments later it was gone, and he turned and followed Teresa and Carmela down the hall.

Twenty-one

As the springtime bloomed on Cypress Avenue, Carlos once again noted how much the weather affected his business. Indeed, how it affected all the business on the Avenue. It seemed everybody was doing better with the nice weather. Of course, he was well aware that Jack was the main reason his own business was good, but he wondered how much Jack, with his infectious good humor, might have been responsible for the increase in the other merchants' business as well.

April was coming to an end, and it looked like the downside of spring was going to be as beautiful as the upside had been. As the sun rose higher in the sky, the morning warmed, and it seemed more like a midsummer's day than the sixth week of spring. Carlos couldn't remember when he'd been this content with his life. Having a few people waiting at his door in

The Journeyman and the Apprentice

the morning and staying that busy throughout the rest of the day was now a regular occurrence. And he was getting so much done with his music. Teresa's day job at Gateway was really working out great for both of them. Life couldn't be better.

Jack's business was booming, too. And he was happy with his new family. He wasn't married into it yet, but that was coming, and he knew he could wait. In the meantime he was building a nest egg for that future time when Carmela would graduate from college and they'd be married. For her part she couldn't be happier. She loved being a full-time student and was so glad to no longer be working at a menial job.

Señora Guevara was just plain content because of everybody else's happiness.

Enrique Contreras was also one of the beneficiaries of the newfound commercial growth on Cypress Avenue since Jack's arrival. Just as Carlos' business was growing, so also was Enrique's. The two men rarely read the Eight Star together anymore because they were both so busy, but they saw each other almost everyday after Carlos closed the shop and he'd go over to buy a couple bottles of Eastside for him and Jack. A couple or three times a week

Enrique would lock up his store, cross the street with Carlos and join the two barbers for an ice-cold beer.

The End

1991-2019

About the Author

Jerome Arthur grew up in Los Angeles, California. He lived on the beach in Belmont Shore, a neighborhood in Long Beach, California, for nine years in the 1960s. He and his wife Janet moved to Santa Cruz, California in 1969. These three cities are the settings for his ten novels.

CPSIA information can be obtained
at www.ICGtesting.com
Printed in the USA
FSHW011820210320
68331FS